My Tricks & Treats

This edition published in 1993 by SMITHMARK Publishers Inc.
16 East 32nd Street, New York NY 10016

© 1993 by Magnolia Editions Limited
Text © 1993 Carin Dewhirst
Illustrations © 1993 Rowan Barnes Murphy
Photographs © 1993 Nancy Palubniak

ISBN 0-8317-5172-X

MY TRICKS AND TREATS
Halloween Stories, Songs, Poems, Recipes, Crafts, and Fun for Kids
was prepared and produced by
Magnolia Editions Limited
15 West 26th Street
New York, NY 10010

Editor: Karla Olson
Art Director: Jeff Batzli
Photography Editor: Anne K. Price
Production Manager: Jeanne E. Kaufman
Line Illustrations by Tayna Ross Hughes

Typeset by Bookworks Plus
Color separations by Bright Arts (Hong Kong) Pte. Ltd.
Printed in Hong Kong and bound in China by Leefung-Asco Printers Ltd.

SMITHMARK Books are available for bulk purchase for sales promotion and premium
use. For details write or call the manager of special sales, SMITHMARK Publishers Inc.,
16 East 32nd Street, New York, NY 10016; (212) 532-6600.

My Tricks & Treats

Halloween Stories, Songs, Poems, Recipes, Crafts, and Fun for Kids

Carin Dewhirst and Joan Dewhirst
Illustrations by Rowan Barnes Murphy
Photographs by Nancy and Jerry Palubniak

SMITHMARK

Contents

Introduction

HALLOWEEN IS IN THE AIR AGAIN! IT'S IN THE WIND THAT POUNCES AND gusts. It's in the pumpkins and the fallen leaves. It's in the darkness where danger lurks. And it's in your thoughts as you plan what you will be for Halloween.

Have you ever wondered why Halloween is so spooky? Or who started carving faces on pumpkin? Or where witches and black cats came from? *My Tricks & Treats* will let you in on all the secrets of Halloween – and much more.

These pages will inspire you to make recipes and crafts such as Sweet Ghosties and Mystery Masks. After reading the scary and sometimes funny Halloween tales, you might even want to have a ghost story–telling party. *My Tricks & Treats* gives you party ideas, suggestions for costumes and food, lots of silly poems and songs, and juicy facts about Halloween. With *My Tricks & Treats* and your imagination, you will have the best Halloween ever!

CHAPTER ONE

Fright Night

Why is Halloween such a frightening night, different from any other? No one really knows, but we do know that it has almost always been a creepy night.

It may have started more than two thousand years ago with the Celts (kelts), a farming tribe that lived in parts of Europe and England. Every year the Celts held a festival called Samhain (SAH-win), and Halloween gets its date and its spookiness from that ancient celebration.

Samhain was the Celts' new year, though they celebrated it on November 1 instead of January 1, as we do. Just as with our New Year's, the celebrating started on the night before or the last night of their year—October 31.

Samhain represented the Celts' new year because it was the last night of summer—the end of the growing and grazing season—and also the beginning of winter and a new farming year. Samhain was that special night between the hot season and the cold.

The Celts worshiped many gods and believed in all sorts of spirits. The rest of the year the spirits stayed in the otherworld or the land of the dead, but on the eve of Samhain—October 31—the barriers between the otherworld and the human world were weak. Large troops of magical beings emerged from burial mounds, hills, lakes, streams, rivers, and springs. Celtic myths tell of fierce monsters going on destructive rampages, using poison or fire to destroy whatever was in their path. The wild destruction of crops, animals, and people could continue all year unless the Celts properly soothed the gods and spirits.

It was a frightening night for the Celts. They used huge fires and magic to protect themselves from these evil spirits and gave them all kinds of gifts. Their religious leaders, called Druids (DROO-ids), lit bonfires on hilltops and gathered deep

*Darkness descends
  On October 31st—
By the light of the moon*

*Imagination takes flight
On a witch's broom. . . .*

*Ghosts and goblins dance
On their midnight spree. . . .*

*Frightening fun begins
On Halloween!*

Seein' Things

Sometimes they're in the corner,
  sometimes they're by the door,

Sometimes they're all a-standin'
  in the middle uv the floor;

Sometimes they are a-sittin' down,
  sometimes they're walkin' round

So softly and so creepylike they never
  make a sound!

Sometimes they are as black as ink
  an' other times they're white—

But the color ain't no difference when
  you see things at night!

—Eugene Field

The Man in the Moon

The Man in the Moon as he sailed in
the sky

Was a very remarkable skipper,

But he made a mistake

When he tried to take

A drink of milk from the Dipper.

He dipped right into the Milky Way

And slowly and carefully filled it.

The Big Bear growled

And the little Bear howled,

And frightened him so he spilled it.

Mister Bones

He dances in the moonlight
  Moments after midnight.
This spindly, skeletal delight
  Known as Mister Bones.

He dances on the gravestones
  Rattling his long bones.
Ignoring ghosts with grim groans
  Merry Mister Bones.

He has a syncopated beat,
  Marking time with his bony feet.
Halloween's the time to meet
  Famous Mister Bones.

in forests under branches of sacred mistletoe. They threw offerings into the bonfires and repeated special charms and spells. All these rituals ensured that crops would grow, animals would multiply, and that they would be safe from evil spirits throughout the coming year.

The Celts celebrated the feast of Samhain for hundreds of years until they were conquered by the Romans in the year A.D. 43. The Romans had a festival to honor the dead called Feralia (fur-AL-ee-ah), and it was also celebrated on October 31. The Romans' festival of Feralia and the Celtic feast of Samhain blended together to make October 31 a double night of the dead.

For many years, people in parts of Europe and England continued to believe that spirits of the dead returned to earth on the night of October 31. Every year they built bonfires and offered gifts to the visiting spirits. A new religion called Christianity was becoming more popular, however, and by the year A.D. 325, it was the official religion of the Roman Empire. Church leaders wanted all religious celebrations to be Christian, but they could not stop people from celebrating the return of the dead on October 31. So the church leaders gave the tradition a new meaning and a new name. These celebrations were now to honor spirits of Christian saints or holy people. The new Christian name was All Saints' Day or All Hallow's Day ("saint" and "hallow" mean the same thing), and the night before was called All Hallow's Even or Halloween.

The night of October 31 was now a time to think about and pray for the spirits of the holy saints who would be visiting the earth on November 1. However, some of the Celts' beliefs emerge again every Halloween, when spirits fly on Fright Night.

Why do we dress up on Halloween? Some say the Celts started it. The Celts wore costumes made from animal heads and furs to the Samhain bonfires. These disguises confused evil spirits, for they did not recognize that a human was beneath the mask, but thought it was another spirit. Evil spirits did not attack other spirits, so the disguised person was safe from harm.

We probably get our custom of wearing masks on Halloween from the Celts, too. During many rituals, including those held on October 31, Celtic priests and priestessess wore metal masks. These masks symbolized gods or goddesses—the priest spoke on behalf of the god when wearing the mask.

Brownies with "Bone Chips"

White chocolate "bone chips" make these fright-night bites especially irresistible. To make them absolutely *good enough to die for*, try this cooking trick: cut the brownies into small squares and freeze them. Defrost them and serve—they will be even moister and more chocolatey!

INGREDIENTS FOR *16* BROWNIES:

1/4 pound butter (1 stick)

1 cup sugar

1/2 cup all-purpose flour

2 ounces (squares) unsweetened chocolate

2 eggs, at room temperature

1 teaspoon vanilla extract

1/3 cup "bone chips" (white chocolate chips)

1. Preheat oven to 350 degrees F. Butter a 9-inch-square baking pan.

2. Place sugar and flour in a medium-sized bowl. Set aside.

3. Melt unsweetened chocolate and butter in a double boiler over low heat on the stove or in a microwave oven. Stir melted mixture until thoroughly mixed.

4. Add melted mixture to the sugar and flour and beat well.

5. Add eggs and vanilla and beat again.

6. Stir in "bone chips."

7. Pour into buttered pan. Bake for 25 to 30 minutes. Do not overbake. These moist brownies might appear too soft in the center, but they will become firmer as they cool.

8. Cool and cut the brownies into squares.

The House on the Corner

The house on the corner had been for sale for over a year. Many people had come to look at it, and several families even wanted to buy it. However, the moment a serious buyer appeared, one of the neighbors felt it was only fair to warn them about the house. "We think the former owners were witches. You wouldn't have believed the parties they had under that old oak tree in the front yard. All dressed in black, chanting nonsense, and dancing around till all hours," one neighbor would whisper. "And we think their spirits still live there," another would add. "We've seen lights going on and off at peculiar times, and I've heard strange clanking and moaning noises in the basement and attic. Now we all call it 'the haunted house.'"

Andy lived two blocks away, and every day he walked his dog Jake past the haunted house. The dog loved to romp and play on the front lawn and sniff about the knobby trunk of the oak tree. One evening, Jake went to the tree for his usual sniff. All of a sudden, he let out a howl such as Andy had never heard before and began to dig furiously at the ground beneath the oak. "Jake, stop! Come here!" Andy yanked on the leash, but Jake kept on digging and kicking up dirt. Suddenly he stopped, worked his head into the hole he'd made, and came out with something in his mouth. He took off then, jerking the leash from Andy's hand.

Andy chased Jake, but trailed him by several yards. He was completely out of breath by the time he reached home, where Jake lay panting on the porch, guarding something with his front paws. "Let me see what you've got, Jake!" Andy ordered. Jake growled and leaped up, took the mysterious object in his mouth, and headed for the backyard. "All right, be that way," Andy yelled, and went inside, leaving the door ajar, in hopes the dog would eventually come in.

A while later, after Jake calmed down, he came into the house and laid his treasure at Andy's feet. It looked like an ordinary bone, but it was unusually smooth and white. Andy reached for the bone, but Jake growled and bared his teeth. "Jake, what has gotten into you?" Fed up with the dog, Andy went into the den to watch television .

A while later, Andy went into the kitchen to make some popcorn. He switched on the light and found Jake with the bone lying by his water dish. Andy stayed away from the bone and Jake stayed by his dish. As the kernels popped and the corn aroma filled the kitchen, Andy heard the first drops of rain pelt the kitchen windows. Jake looked up at Andy with worried eyes. "Don't worry, Jake," Andy said with a laugh. "It's only a little

rain." Suddenly a flash of lightning exploded into the kitchen and made Andy jump. He dropped the pot he'd been shaking and it clanked to the floor, as booming thunder shook the house. Jake bolted from the kitchen as the lights in the house flickered and went out.

"Jake!" Andy screamed, paralyzed with terror and unable to see a thing. He held out his hands to feel his way out of the kitchen. His body ached with fear. He tripped over the fallen pot and sent it knocking against a table leg, which sent another bolt of terror through his limbs. He stumbled into the hallway and practically fell over Jake. His fear melted instantly as he knelt down and hugged the big Labrador. "Good boy, Jake!"

After a moment Andy fumbled in the hall closet, where his parents kept a flashlight. Feeling more secure behind the beam of light, he and Jake scrambled into the den and huddled together on the couch. They watched the rain from the den window, as thunder boomed and lightning flashed around them. Andy shined the flashlight on the overflowing birdbath and the gushing rain gutters, then he opened the window slightly, and the smell of moist, earthy air rushed in. Suddenly Jake perked up his ears. "What is it, Jake?" Andy whispered.

He heard the noise a second later, a low, distant wail, soft and constant like a deep hum. It could have been the wind moaning against the eaves, but there was no wind. Quickly, Andy shut the window.

With the hair on his back standing up, Jake dug between the cushions of the couch and snatched the bone. He held it between his paws. Then he answered the distant eerie moan with his own low, rumbling growl.

"It's only a coyote or some dog howling. Relax, Jakey." Andy reached out to pet him, but Jake moved away and stood as if ready to attack. Andy realized the dog sensed danger—or something. "Come on, Jake, let's call Mom and Dad," he said with a trembling voice.

Andy found the number near the phone where his parents always left it, but when he picked up the receiver the phone was dead. "Great! The power's out and so is the phone." His voice quavered. He fiddled hopelessly with the buttons. Then he did hear something—but it wasn't a dial tone. It was the low, murmuring moan—now more than a hum—getting stronger and closer. Andy strained to listen, wondering if he could make out distinct words. Jake suddenly barked furiously, with the bone secured under a front paw. "No one's going to take your silly bone, Jake," Andy said. "Stop barking!"

Suddenly, Andy could hear words in the low moaning: "Give me my bo-o-o-ne, give me my bo-o-o-ne." A slap of thunder punctuated the low cry.

Jake bristled and clenched the bone in his jaw. Andy and the dog dashed upstairs to Andy's bedroom. They slammed the door and scrambled into the bed, with the covers drawn up to their necks. The deep moan grew even louder and closer. It groaned, "Give me my bo-o-o-o-ne!" Jake whined and Andy pulled the blankets in tighter.

Jake raised his head expectantly as he and Andy heard a creaking sound along with the moaning, coming closer and louder, "Give me my bo-o-one!" Andy pulled Jake to him and drew the covers over his head. The moaning, very close and clear, continued, "Give me my bo-o-o-o-ne!"

Andy and Jake cowered under the bedclothes, too terrorized to peek out. Andy tried not to shake; Jake's fur stood up on his back. The moaning seemed to be just outside the door. Then they heard something drag itself along the bedroom floor, scraping closer and closer to Andy's bed. The voice groaned again, "Give me my *b-o-o-o-ne!*"

Something jostled the bed. Andy's heart raced and Jake's whole body shook. The booming voice was directly overhead and it echoed against the walls of the room, *"Give me my bo-o-o-o-ne!"*

Andy snatched the bone away from Jake. He sat straight up in bed and flung the object toward the window. He shouted into the frightening air, *"Take it!"* as the bone crashed through the glass.

Jake and Andy heard a loud sucking noise, as they were pulled from the bed, covers and all, and dumped onto the middle of the bedroom floor. The boy and his dog crouched together for a moment more. The sound grew more and more distant, until all they heard was the pounding rain. Feeling weak, Andy rose and went to the window. Down in the yard he could see the broken glass. Whatever had moved through the yard had toppled the birdbath, trampled shrubs, and uprooted trees. The bone was nowhere in sight. Both Andy and Jake hoped they would never see it again.

Mystery Masks

Create mystery by wearing a mask! For a change of pace, these masks are hand-held—you don't have to worry about wearing an uncomfortable mask that might also block your vision. Don't limit yourself to decorating with paint and glitter—try using dried leaves, moss, and twigs.

This mask pattern is simple, but let your imagination soar and transform the simple into the simply wondrous! You can make a mask to cover just your eyes, or one that covers your entire face.

MATERIALS:

8 1/2-by-11-inch piece of paper

heavy paper plate

cardboard tube from a wire pant hanger

glue or spray adhesive (but ask an adult to help you with this)

scissors

pencil

STEPS:

Eye Mask

1. *Fold, Draw, and Cut:* Fold the paper in half and draw a mask pattern as shown. Cut out and unfold.

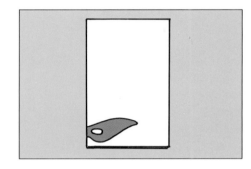

2. *Trace and Cut:* Trace around pattern onto paper plate. Cut out.

3. *Glue and Let Dry:* With a large dab of glue, attach the cardboard tube onto the mask at the edge of one side. Let it dry thoroughly.

Face Mask

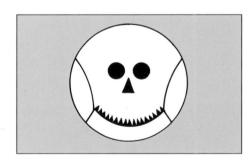

1. *Draw and Cut:* Draw face mask pattern onto plate as shown. Cut out.

2. *Glue and Let Dry:* With a large dab of glue, attach the cardboard tube onto the mask at the bottom edge . Let it dry thoroughly.

DECORATING:

Skull Mask

Make a full-face mask and paint it white. Make eyes from an egg carton. Add cotton hair and paint.

Moss Mask

Use the eye mask pattern. Paint the entire mask light green, then brush with glue and add moss. Good for forest fairies.

Silver Mask

Can be used for princess or wizard. Use fabric paint to make raised designs. Apply the fabric paint first, let it dry, then spray with paint. Brush on glue and sprinkle with glitter.

Leaf Mask

Collect dried leaves or purchase cloth ones at a craft store. Apply leaves with dabs of glue.

Black Mask with Feathers

Use the eye mask pattern. Paint it black. Let it dry. Glue feathers to the back of the mask. When the mask is completely dry, paint it again with glue and sprinkle on black glitter. Outline the eye holes with red glitter fabric paint.

Gold Mask

Use the eye mask pattern. Glue on small Christmas tree ornaments or other small balls. Let it dry. Use fabric paint to outline the edge of mask and eye holes. Let it dry. Paint the entire mask with gold paint.

SKULL MASK

MOSS MASK

SILVER MASK

LEAF MASK

GOLD MASK

BLACK GLITTER MASK

CHAPTER TWO

Ghosts, Ghosts, Ghosts

It is said that on Halloween night, in graveyards everywhere, a bizarre ritual takes place. At exactly midnight, Death raps on tombstones and awakens dead souls. Ghosts, specters, phantoms, shades, spooks, and apparitions all gracefully materialize above the graves. The music starts— tunes that can't be heard by the living—and the transparent figures dance in circles faster and faster until they are a blurred cloud of haunted motion.

Then suddenly the dancing stops. As the first rays of morning light reach the horizon, the ghostly dancers fade into the quiet, cold tombs and silent graves. The spirits will return the next Halloween at midnight, when Death rouses them once again for another dance of the dead.

Halloween is a special night for spirits of the dead. The ancient Celts, from whom we get Halloween, probably started this spooky tradition. The Celts believed that good and evil spirits were everywhere on the night of October 31, the eve of their big feast of Samhain. The Celts lived more than two thousand years ago, but we still think of nothing but ghosts, ghosts, ghosts on Halloween night.

If you want to see a ghost, you need to know what you are looking for, and you must have proper equipment. Professional ghost hunters are called psychic (SEYE-kik) researchers. They investigate places that are thought to be haunted. Psychic researchers try to record the presence of a ghost using special infrared cameras that can take pictures in the dark, and other electronic equipment that measures the "psychic energy" of ghosts.

Even if you are not a psychic researcher, you can still look for ghosts. Ghosts usually haunt a place of death, such as a battlefield, the site of a plane crash, or the location of a murder or accidental death. Graveyards are said to be haunted by

Is your house haunted?
Check for these warning signs:

Do you hear strange, unexplainable bumping and thumping noises coming from the attic?

Are there bloodstains that reappear after you have cleaned them up?

Do muddy footprints leading to the attic mysteriously appear?

Are you often awakened by the violent rattling of the crystal chandelier?

If you answered "yes" to any of the above, get out of your house fast!

Spooky Ghouls' Bonfire Ball

Come dance to the music of Four
  Owls and Their Hoots

Songs by Three Croaking Frogs in
  green suits;

Everyone's invited, those who have
  the gall,

To the Spooky Ghouls' Bonfire Ball.

Make no mistake, choose a clever
  disguise;

There will be a contest with a serious
  prize.

The most terrifying costume will win
  it all

At the Spooky Ghouls' Bonfire Ball.

Grab your capes, put on your
  mustaches;

Slip into your gowns, glue on your
  false lashes.

Trek deep in the forest to Tree Trunk
  Hall,

For the Spooky Ghouls' Bonfire Ball.

Witches will concoct a smooth and
  dangerous brew;

Vampires will cook up a hearty, very
  tasty stew.

Then you'll disappear forever, leaving
  no clues at all

Of the Spooky Ghouls' Bonfire Ball.

Ghosts
(To the tune of "Merrily We Roll Along")

Eerily they glide along, slide along,
  glide along.

Eerily they glide along, ghosts out on
  a spree.

only one ghost: the spirit of the first person to be buried there (except on Halloween, when others are invited to dance there). This type of ghost is called a graveyard guardian, and it protects the burial ground from evil spirits and intruders.

Phantoms or ghosts are not that difficult to recognize because they usually seem to be made of a pale, white mist. Unlike the living, they can appear and disappear whenever they want to and can pass through walls and doors. We usually think of ghosts wearing white hooded capes—and some do. These are graveyard ghosts and they appear wearing their long, flowing burial robes called shrouds (shrowds). Other ghosts wear the clothes in which they died or were buried.

If you are looking for ghosts, there's no telling what type you might see. You might come across a haunting ghost, one that is always seen at the same place. This type of ghost pays little attention to living people, it is attracted only to the place where it died. You might see the ghost of a living person who is in great danger or near death. These ghosts appear only once. Some ghosts materialize to deliver a message or a warning to the living. Like most ghosts, these do not speak, but make signs to explain the message.

There are many old stories about ghosts who have special jobs. In Shakespeare's *Hamlet,* the ghost of Hamlet's father appears to expose his own murderer. Some ghosts appear to reveal the hiding place of money or treasure, or to make certain that property or money is returned to its rightful owner. If a person was particularly bad while alive, that person's ghost might return to earth to make amends.

Poltergeists (POHL-ter-geyests) are noisy, silly ghosts. A poltergeist might cause objects to fly through the air or make loud noises, but these spirits mean no real harm. Poltergeist activity happens most often around people ages twelve to sixteen. Some say that a poltergeist is not really a ghost—it's a special energy or power called psychokinesis (seye-koh-ki-NEE- sis). This energy comes from the minds of young people and it is responsible for poltergeist activity.

Listen for ghosts. Some legends say that they make feeble squeaking sounds like mice or chirping birds.

You might find a gallows ghost at a crossroads. Long ago, a crossroads was considered a good place to hang a criminal, because the victim's ghost would be confused by all the roads, and would be unable to take revenge on its executioners.

No matter where they are, ghosts are tricky and eerie. Watch your step or you might get caught in a swirling, ghostly mist.

Sweet Ghosties

If all ghosts were as sweet as these ghosties, everyone would want to live in a haunted house. Just like real ghosts, these marshmallow-and-popcorn spooks have been known to disappear quickly. So, cooks beware!—have some extras on hand. For variation, make some Sweet Ghosties with eerie chocolate eyes and others with red, beady gumdrop eyes.

INGREDIENTS FOR EIGHT GHOSTIES:

7 cups plain popped popcorn

2 1/2 cups puffed rice cereal (not crispy rice cereal)

4 cups miniature marshmallows

6 tablespoons butter or margarine

16 chocolate morsels or red gumdrops

Waxed paper

1 tablespoon softened butter for hands

1. Mix popcorn and cereal in a large bowl with your hands.

2. Melt butter or margarine over low heat. Add marshmallows and stir until melted. Remove from heat.

3. Dribble melted mixture over popcorn and cereal and stir with wooden spoon until evenly coated.

4. Rub a little butter on your hands. When popcorn-cereal mix is cool to the touch, take a handful and form it into a ghostly shape, as shown. Flatten it at the bottom and place on waxed paper. Add chocolate morsels or gumdrop eyes.

Ghosts are an international phenomenon!

According to Japanese legends, ghosts were deformed as punishment for evil deeds committed when they were living. These ghosts must wander forever with their legs constantly on fire.

In Italy there is a 400-year-old legend of a glowing ghost who can foretell death.

In India, hordes of small, red demon ghosts called bautas (BOW-tahs) roam around attacking people with their sharp, pointed teeth.

General Morris

Not long before he died, old General Morris realized that his relatives wanted his fortune. He knew the night he gave a party in honor of his new and very young wife, Sybil. At the table, General Morris raised his glass and announced, "When our first-born child comes of age, he or she will be the sole heir to the entire Morris fortune!" Sybil blushed with joy, but the aunts, uncles, and cousins grew pale with disappointment. They cast sinister looks at Sybil that clearly said, "If only you had not come along, young lady, then the fortune would be ours!"

General Morris knew that his relatives would do anything to get his money, so he hid it carefully. On his deathbed, he told Sybil where to find the treasure and asked her to guard it until their newborn son, James, came of age.

For almost eighteen years, Sybil protected James's inheritance. Then several months before James was to inherit the fortune, General Morris's cousins, Pauline and Wilton, came for a visit—and things got out of hand.

Wilton and Pauline were the worst kind of guests and James disliked them thoroughly. They yelled at the servants, demanding dinner on the table *now*. They gobbled their food, and careless Wilton broke a crystal goblet at almost every meal—he never once apologized. They insisted on being taken here and there, never asking Sybil and James what they wanted to do. And they stayed for three interminable weeks.

One morning near the end of the third week, Wilton suggested that he and James go on a two-day duck-hunting trip. James reluctantly accepted.

After several hours in the duck blind waiting patiently for the birds and not speaking to each other, Wilton suddenly asked James a question.

"You'll soon be a very rich man," he said. "What are you going to do with all your money?"

James shifted awkwardly. "Well, I'm not sure, really. I haven't thought about it much yet. I guess my mother has some ideas. . . ."

Wilton interrupted rudely. "Your mother knows nothing about money! Sybil can't manage the Morris fortune. What has she done with it all these years? Has she made investments? Bought real estate? Stocks? Bonds?" Wilton swept his arms dramatically with each word. "Tell me, James, what has she done to increase your wealth?"

Wilton could sense he was frightening James with his strong words, so he changed his tone. He made his voice as sweet as honey and put his arm around James's shoulder.

"I know a lot about financial matters, James, and I would be more than happy to

help you manage your money. Just tell me where to find the fortune and put your mind at ease. I'll handle everything." Wilton smiled insincerely at James.

Before James could respond, they both heard the Morris chauffeur running through the woods. In moments, agitated and out of breath, he was in the duck blind.

"Sirs, there's trouble at Morris Mansion. You must return immediately. Miss Pauline did not tell me why, but you must hurry!"

Wilton and James rushed back to the mansion, then instinctively ran to Sybil's room. Pauline sat at Sybil's bedside. She moved away from the bed as the men entered and started whispering with Wilton in a corner of the room.

As James sat with his dying mother, he caught snatches of Wilton and Pauline's whispering. "I called you back because if James doesn't know where the fortune is, I think she will tell him with her last breath. I know I said not to bring him back until she was dead, but this is our only chance since *you* couldn't get the information out of him."

James leaped away from the bed and grabbed Pauline by her shoulders and shook her. "What have you done to her?" he screamed.

Suddenly, Sybil let out a long breath, and her eyes focused on James. "James, the treasure, it's . . ." she expelled. Both James and Pauline ran for the bed and crouched near Sybil. Pauline tried to push her face between Sybil's and James's so she could hear the dying woman's words. But before Sybil spoke again, she gasped and her body became rigid. She stared wide-eyed at James for an instant, then went limp.

James cried, "No, Mother, please . . ." He shook her gently, trying to awaken her.

From across the room, Wilton spoke with a knowing grin. "She's gotten no more than she deserves, boy, leave her be," he cackled with a sneer. Wilton and Pauline laughed.

James lunged at them, but Wilton stopped him with a powerful blow that knocked James to the floor.

James was disoriented when he finally woke up, but the unfamiliar faded into the familiar, and he realized he was in the room where his father had died. As he got up, he winced, for his head pounded with pain. He walked to the window and looked down into the mansion's cemetery. Then his heart ached, for he saw several people standing by a fresh grave, his mother's grave. How he wanted to avenge her death! He went and kicked and pounded on the locked door, but it wouldn't budge. He leaned his throbbing head against the door and heard a commotion downstairs, a distant, constant pounding and periodic laughter. James went to another window and saw several cars in the driveway and he realized what was going on. Since Pauline and Wilton could not find the Morris fortune, they had invited the other greedy relatives over for a treasure hunt.

James surveyed the room again; there was no way out and he knew it. He sat hopelessly on the bed, resting his head in his hands.

What was he going to do, for his mother had not been able to tell him where the fortune was hidden. James raised his head and his gaze met that of his father staring down from his portrait. James pleaded with his father's likeness for help.

James wondered if he was dreaming for he heard the rattling of medals and then the ringing sound of a metal sword. He looked nervously about the room, then raised his eyes again to the portrait. With a rustling, General Morris stepped from the portrait and stood before his son. He smiled warmly, then motioned for James to follow him. The door opened magically, and they walked downstairs.

They followed the pounding and the laughter to the dining room where Pauline, Wilton, and the others were gathered. Some were feasting on the meats, cheeses, and fruit heaped on the table. Others, such as Wilton, held large goblets of wine, and all were busy with hammers and picks. Wilton was trying to dig up the floor near the fireplace. Pauline directed several other cousins to remove all the paintings and tapestries from the walls. They were now chipping away at the plaster, looking frantically for hollow cubbies in the wall where the treasure might be hidden.

James looked over at his father's ghost, and the ghost smiled broadly. Suddenly a bitter wind whipped through the dining room and rattled the chandeliers. Everyone stopped talking and their tools clattered to the stone floor. They looked at each other fearfully, then Wilton said, "It was only the wind, a window must have blown open somewhere. Carry on. Remember, there's a bonus for whoever finds the fortune first."

Pauline moved uncertainly to the fireplace and Wilton joined her. They conversed in whispers for several minutes, trying to decide where to tell their hardworking crew to look next. Suddenly, a huge burst of flames was unleashed by the fire: Pauline shrieked and Wilton screamed as they were enveloped by the flames. All the relatives stood by, watching in terror, as Pauline and Wilton were consumed.

Their mesmerized terror was broken when platters of food suddenly rose from the table and began spinning wildly overhead. Evil aunts were dunked with ladles full of gravy. Conniving cousins were pelted with buttered potatoes, string beans, and dollops of chocolate pudding. Unsavory uncles were slapped with sliced turkey and batted with meatballs. Everyone screamed and headed for the front door, but before they could get there the hole in the floor where they had been pounding gaped open, swallowed every single greedy relative, then closed again with no sign of disrepair.

General Morris's ghost turned to James and winked. He picked up a candelabrum from the table and magically lit each taper with his index finger. His gentle eyes twinkled, and he beckoned for James to follow him again.

The ghost led James from room to room and showed him where the Morris fortune was hidden, right under the relatives' noses. Jewels were embedded in the picture frames—the very frames Pauline had cast aside. Gold and silver had been woven into the tapestries—tapestries Wilton had carelessly pulled from the walls. The general's ghost showed James secret drawers where money, gems, and title deeds were hidden.

Finally, they returned to the room where the general had died and stood before the fireplace. The ghost reached out to place a reassuring hand on James's shoulder, when a distant clock chimed and the ghost vanished into his portrait on the wall.

Flowing Capes

A flowing cape will make you feel truly dressed up. Choose materials such as old sheets, slinky silver fabric, or satiny black and red cloth to get the effect you want. With this pattern you can make a ghost, dracula, witch, or princess cape—all are quite dashing and fun to wear. Get help from an adult for this project, as you will be using a hot iron and doing some sewing.

Ghostly Getup

This is a super-easy cape to make. Use a regular white bed sheet, or a flannel sheet for a softer cape. With white face paint and a bit of dark eye makeup you will be the ghost of your dreams—or your nightmares!

STEPS:

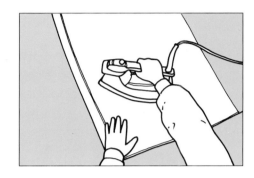

1. *Iron:* Place fusible adhesive, paper side up, on stitching line of largest hem edge of sheet. Preheat iron to medium heat and ask someone to help you iron the adhesive to the sheet. When fabric is cool, peel off paper backing.

2. *Fold and Press:* To make a nice, big hood, fold over the top edge of sheet 24 inches. Press the folded edge with iron to bond the fabric together. Make a casing by sewing along the stitching line of largest hem edge of sheet; stitch again one inch below that line.

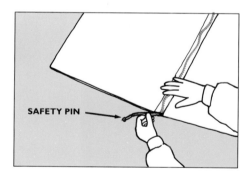

SAFETY PIN →

3. *Thread Cord:* Put a large safety pin through one end of the cord. Push the pin through the hem and draw up to make the ghost cape.

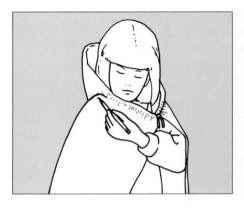

4. *Measure and Cut:* Try on cape. It should be at least 8 inches above the ground, so you can walk easily. Cut off at bottom edge if necessary. Mark with a pencil at the top of your arms and cut two slits for armholes. Roll back edge of hood if it is too deep.

Slinky Ghost

Use a twin bed–size flat sheet and two yards of silver fabric. Pin them together, right sides facing each other. Stitch along both ends and down one long edge. Trim seams, turn right-side out, and press. Make a casing by stitching 17 inches down from top; stitch again one inch above that stitch line. Thread cord through casing and pull to gather cape.

Dracula Cape

Use 2 yards each of red and black satin fabric. Pin right sides of fabric together, and stitch along both ends and down one long edge. Trim seams, turn right-side out, and press. To make Dracula's stiff collar: Fold cape in half across. Make a point 12 inches down from top edge and 5 inches from fold. Place a pin at this point on both sides of cape. Make a casing by stitching 12 inches down from collar edge and up to pin marker. Repeat stitching 1 inch above first stitch line. Insert a piece of thin cardboard 9 by 9 inches in the center slit between casing stitching—don't forget to finish the casing stitching between the pin markers. Thread black cord through casing and draw up.

Witch Cape

Follow the steps for the Dracula cape, but use all black fabric.

Princess Cape

Use 3 yards of pink tulle or net; 1/2 yard each of several other colors of net; 2 yards of 2-inch-wide pink satin ribbon. Cut the smaller pieces of net into 6-inch squares. Fold pink net in half. Make casing by stitching 8 inches down from folded edge and 2 inches above that stitching line. Lay cape on floor and glue net pieces in various color patterns near neck edge of cape. Let dry overnight. Thread satin ribbon through casing and pull up.

Three Little Ghostesses

Three little ghostesses,
Sitting on postesses,
Eating buttered toastesses,
Greasing their fistesses,
Up to their wristesses,
Oh, what beastesses
To make such feastesses!

CHAPTER THREE

How to Recognize a Witch

Dark, sinister figures, dressed all in black with tall pointy hats, hang over a huge bubbling pot. Through the foul-smelling fumes, their eyes glow red in their greenish faces. Withered hands stir the boiling broth while throaty cackles and chants fill the mixture with trouble, mischief, and evil. Beware . . . these are the wicked witches, and tonight is their special night. It's Halloween! One of them will come to meet you, if you follow these directions: Put your clothes on wrong side out and walk backward to a place where two roads cross each other. At the stroke of midnight, she'll be there. Look out! She might change you into a toad!

There was a time, many years ago, when people in all parts of the world believed in witches and witchcraft. The first witches were both men and women, young and old. They were presumed to have supernatural power, but it was not always used for evil purposes. "Good" witches created magical cures with carefully concocted herbal medicines and produced protective charms and highly successful love potions. Some had the ability to tell fortunes and predict the future.

"Evil" witches did lots of mean and nasty things, such as stir up violent storms, give people diseases, or make milk taste sour and awful. They also concocted powerful potions in giant cauldrons using such gruesome ingredients as slimy snake filets and ugly eyes of toads. These were used as poisons to get rid of enemies.

Double, double, toil and trouble;
Fire burn and cauldron bubble.

For a charm of powerful trouble,
Like a hell-broth boil and bubble.

—MACBETH, SHAKESPEARE

Queen of the Witches

Hecate, Hecate this old witch.

She brews potions thick as pitch.

Casts her spells without a glitch.

Hecate, Hecate this old witch.

Halloween Chant

Heyhow for Hallowe'en,
When all the witches are to be seen.
Some in black and some in green,
Heyhow for Hallowe'en.

Three Witches

Halloween, the night of screams,
Three witches looking mean,
One black and one green,
And one crying, "Halloween!"

Magic Charm

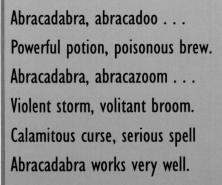

Abracadabra, abracadoo . . .
Powerful potion, poisonous brew.
Abracadabra, abracazoom . . .
Violent storm, volitant broom.
Calamitous curse, serious spell
Abracadabra works very well.

"Abracadabra" is the oldest spoken charm we know. It occurs in a poem written in Latin at the beginning of the second century.

"Volitant" means engaged in or having the power of flight.

"Good" witches were able to break the spells of "evil" witches. However, most people were afraid of all witches because they believed their mystical powers came from the devil. Among these special powers was the ability of some witches to transform themselves into other shapes, mainly cats. Whenever people saw a cat, they would ask, "Is this really a cat, or a witch changed into a cat?"

Witches held two very gala celebrations, or sabbats (SAB-bats), every year. The first was on the eve of May Day and was called Roodmas (ROOD-mahs) in England and Walpurgis Nacht (vahl-pur-GISS-nahkt) in Germany. The other occurred on October 31, our present-day Halloween. These secret get-togethers featured lots of feasting and dancing. Attendance was a must for serious witches and required special preparation. First, a witch rubbed herself with a certain "flying" ointment made from baboon's blood, baby fat, and tomb dust. Then she climbed on her broomstick and flew to the secret meeting place, cackling curses to herself.

It was easy in those early days to blame witches for everything that went wrong. Scientific knowledge was limited and when crops failed or animals died, people believed wicked witches had cast their evil spells. Throughout the early Middle Ages, church leaders taught that witchcraft was mainly superstition. However, during the thirteenth century, church authorities decided that witchcraft was in reality a form of devil worship and posed a dangerous threat to Christianity. They declared the practice of witchcraft a crime punishable by death. This initiated a terrible period of witch-hunting that lasted for several hundred years. Many witch-hunter books were written that listed clues to look for in a suspected witch. Clues were things like having warts or moles, or keeping an animal as a pet. (Most of our ideas about witchcraft have come from these manuals.) Thousands of innocent people were forced, by brutal torture, into making false confessions, for which they were killed.

Fact or fiction? Truth or superstition? Do witches really exist? There are people today who call themselves witches. They claim to do unusual tricks and to attend special secret meetings on Halloween. But do they fly? See for yourself, at the crossing of two roads . . . exactly at midnight!

Witches' Brew

Hot

A real witch might make this brew in a cauldron over a roaring bonfire, but you can use a large pot and simmer the brew on the stove. Be sure to stir the brew in "widdershins" or counterclockwise direction the way witches do.

INGREDIENTS FOR 8 MUGS OF HOT BREW:

1 quart sweet apple cider

1 cup orange juice

1/2 cup lemon juice

1 cup pineapple juice

1 stick cinnamon

1/2 teaspoon whole cloves

Honey to taste

1. Combine the ingredients in a suitable cauldron (a large pot). Simmer over low heat until hot, stirring often. Pour into mugs and serve.

Cold

Want to startle your friends? Draw a spider on the outside bottom of a clear plastic tumbler before you pour in the brew. As your friends drink, they will think they are sipping spiders. Watch them squeal!

INGREDIENTS FOR 8 GLASSES OF COLD BREW:

1 6-ounce can frozen lemonade concentrate

1 quart apple juice

1 quart ginger ale or 7-Up

2 cups cranberry juice cocktail

2 cups orange juice

very thin orange slices

1. Combine all ingredients in a large pitcher and chill. Using a semipermanent black marker, draw spiders on the outside bottom of each glass.

2. Pour the cold brew over ice cubes in tall glasses.

3. Cut orange slices and place on lip of each glass.

4. Wait for your friends to scream!

Witches' Brews

Witches' brew hot, witches' brew cold,

Witches brew it in the pot nine days old.

Some like it hot, some like it cold.

No peeking in the pot, 'cause witches will scold!

The cauldron was not only for preparing magic potions. It was used to cook food for the sabbat feasts as well.

Wicked Witching Lessons

Isabelle was scared and nervous. Today was the final test. If she could pass this one, she would have her all-time favorite wish. She would be an ugly, mean, nasty, wicked witch.

She was worried. She thought about some of the classes she had taken: Cosmetic Uglification—Wart Emphasis; Witch Speech 101—Cackling, Screeching, and Hissing; Small Beast Preserving; Writing an Effective or Deadly Spell; Horrid Marinades and Sauces; Basic Broom Design and Repair; Witch Trials and You. She was behind on a lot of her homework assignments—especially Small Beast Preserving. Where was she going to find wombat wings? The teachers reported her progress as slow, but it wasn't because she hadn't made an effort.

Take Poison Potions class, for instance. She followed the basic brewing directions, she just changed the ingredients a little. The final test recipe called for toe of frog. She threw in the leg. She couldn't bear to pull the wings off an owl, so she used chicken instead. They were out of fresh hemlock root and yew slips at the Wicked West Supermarket, so she used fresh basil and green onions. The baboon's blood cost $3,000 an ounce and she needed three ounces, so she bought tomato sauce. (It was the same color and the old nasty witch teacher probably wouldn't even notice.) She brought the mixture to a roaring boil in one of the large school cauldrons and stirred it very carefully in the proper counterclockwise direction. When the brew seemed to be thick enough, Isabelle took a grimy, greasy ladleful and walked over to her witch teacher. Isabelle put on her best witch's scowl and cackled, "Heh, heh, heh, try my delici——I mean, heh, heh, *horrrrid* potion." She made certain she spilled a bit of it on a fellow student as she handed the spoon to her glaring witch teacher. The ugly old hag lifted the ladle to her cracked lips and gulped. Immediately her veiny red eyes bulged and she spat the mouthful right in Isabelle's face. "You failed. It's delicious!"

Things weren't much better in the Witch Stitchery class. The final sewing project was to make a witch's uniform. Isabelle worked on hers for weeks. She made her own pattern and stitched up a basic black cape. It was a little too short, so she added a strip of black lace at the hemline. She sewed secret pockets inside where she could hide small slimy snakes and biting beetles to frighten unsuspecting strangers. She spent days working on her hat. It came out extra-pointy, so she added fur trim at the brim plus some sparkles and a wispy sheer veil. To her spiderweb lace gloves she attached little satin pouches. Perfect for sneezing and itching powder and bus fare, she thought.

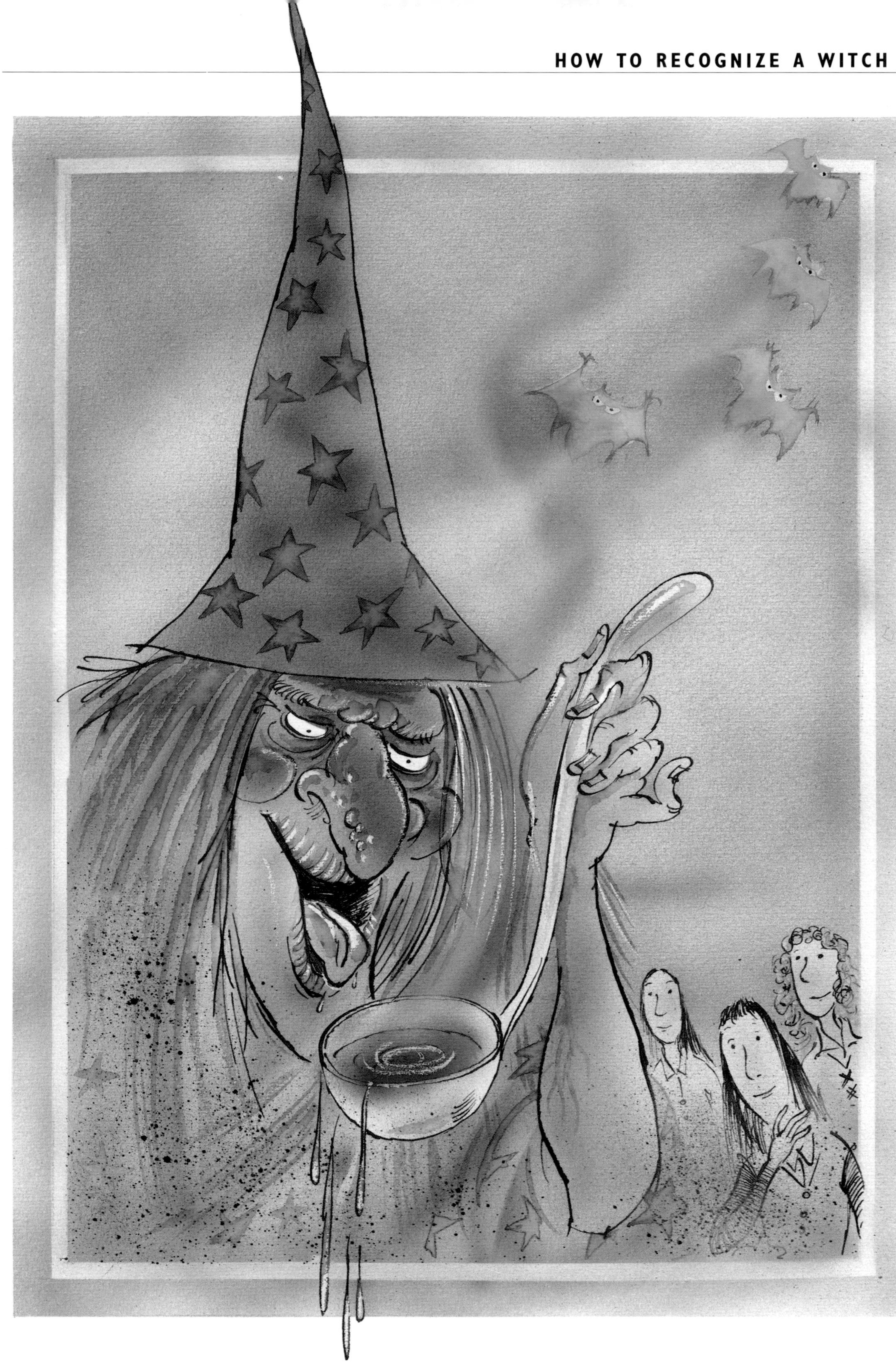

She was nervous getting into her uniform, and her stomach churned while she waited in line to be graded. The witch student in front of her didn't help matters. She looked so awful and smelled so wretched that Isabelle wanted to cry. "She's perfectly wonderful," she muttered to herself. Isabelle was so anxious she couldn't even think of a good nasty spell to cast on her classmate.

Suddenly, it was her turn. Isabelle stepped out in front of the wicked witch teacher, leaned on her broom for support, and let out her best cackle. But the only sound that came out of her throat was a giggle. The witch teacher was furious. Her long bony fingers ripped the fur from Isabelle's hat. She knocked the hat to the ground and stomped it to pieces. Then she screamed, "You failed. You look beautiful!"

Spelling class was also a challenge. She found a fat black fuzzy worm and put it into a jar. She thought she'd change it into a large, hairy spider. "Won't my sister scream when this goes down her back," Isabelle said to herself with a cackle. Unfortunately, she mixed up the Revolting-Insect-Changer spell with the Ravishing-Insect-Changer spell and the chubby worm sprouted huge wings with spots of crimson, sienna, and gold and fluttered about the classroom. The angry witch teacher's face turned red and she waved her scraggly broom in the air trying to bat at it. She missed several times and hit some of the students and also knocked potions and assorted marinating insect parts to the floor. The witch teacher was particularly enraged when the delicate butterfly flew out the classroom window. She screamed and stamped her crooked feet. "You failed! It's lovely, and it got away before I could pick its wings off."

Now Isabelle was worried about the final exam: Broomstick Takeoff, Flying, and Landing. Will I get off the ground? she wondered to herself as she polished her broom handle with Brilliant-Broom wax until it gleamed. She had combed the broom bristles into a sleek thick tuft.

When it was Isabelle's turn to fly, she warmed up the broom properly but instead of hitting the "fly" button, she pressed "circle cycle." There was no takeoff, she just zoomed at the highest speed close to the ground in a wide circle. Before she knew it the dust from the school flying field was in her eyes and she couldn't see the broom control panel. One, two, three classmates were swept off their brooms. Over the buzzing of her broomstick she could hear the screeching and hissing of her classmates. "I've got to slow down!" she cried, and hit the broom control panel. But instead of slowing, the broom went into "hyperflight" and she picked up even more speed. In an instant she had dusted the rest of the class and was gaining on the refreshment table.

Isabelle's broom caught the edge of the ragged black lace tablecloth, and she felt a slimy splash as the bowl of Pond Punch hit the dirt. Now she was headed for the witch teacher! She dug the sharp heels of her witch boots into the ground and started to slow, but the witch teacher wasn't running away fast enough. Isabelle couldn't find the broom brake, and she and her teacher collided in a cloud of witch hats, potions, and dirt.

When the dust settled Isabelle was on the ground next to her still-idling broomstick. Her classmates had formed a screaming, shrieking circle about her. They looked

disheveled and angry. The witch teacher loomed above in her dirty dress and crumpled hat and hissed, "You failed! You're grounded! You'll never be a witch!"

Isabelle got to her feet and brushed the tears from her eyes and the dust from everywhere else. "Please," she begged, "you must give me another chance."

The Witchtress, the head school witch, motioned her to remain in her place. All the witch teachers gathered together on the far edge of the field and spoke in low, raspy whispers. It seemed like hours before the Witchtress returned to where Isabelle was waiting. Isabelle could not help blurting out, "This is all a mistake. I know I could make a very good witch."

The Witchtress nodded her head under its tall sleek hat and croaked, "That is exactly the point. Witches are not meant to be good. Witches are ugly, mean, nasty, and wicked. We make awful potions and cast evil spells. You are much too sweet and beautiful. You could never be a bad witch, full-time. However, we witches have decided to let you be a witch for one night, and one night only, every year."

Isabelle's face brightened a little. "And what night would that be?" she asked, smiling weakly.

"Why, Halloween, of course!" snapped the Witchtress. "And don't smile about it! You're a witch!"

Witch's Hat and More!

A great hat will make your costume. This pattern is easy, but requires a little patience, so take your time. Ask for help if you decide to make a complicated hat such as Princess of Birdland.

Cone-shaped hats aren't just for witches anymore! Leave off the brim and be a wizard, princess, or leaf fairy.

MATERIALS:

large sheet poster board

pencil

scissors

glue (or rubber cement, or spray adhesive—but only if an adult helps you use it)

ruler

stapler

extra sheet posterboard (for brim)

STEPS:

1. *Measure:* Using a piece of string or cloth measuring tape, measure the distance around your head where you want the hat to fit. Make sure the hat doesn't cover your eyes.

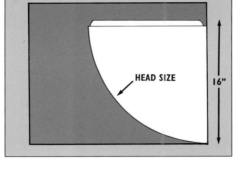

2. *Measure, Draw, and Cut:* Measure 16 inches from the bottom edge of the poster board and make a dot. Draw lines to make a pattern as shown. Make the distance between the two outer lines an arc the same as the mesurement around your head. Cut along the outer edge as shown—don't cut off the little flap.

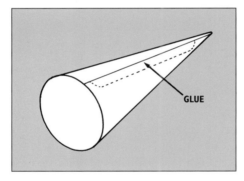

3. *Glue and Roll:* Apply glue to the flap and allow it to dry for a few minutes. Roll the paper into a cone shape by bringing the flap to meet the other edge of the poster board just like the picture. The outer edge of the poster board without the flap should meet the line. Glue flap to the underside of the poster board.

4. *Staple and Hold:* Staple at the bottom and hold cone in place for a few minutes until the glue sets.

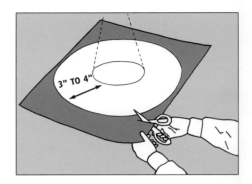

5. *Add Brim:* Add a brim if you are making a witch's hat. Trace around the bottom of the cone shape. Use a ruler and mark about 3 to 4 inches all around the circle. Draw a larger circle around the inner one. Cut out around the larger, outer circle.

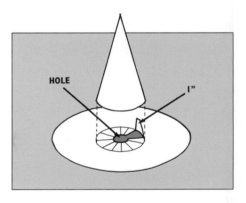

6. *Punch Hole and Cut:* Cut a small hole in the center of the circle, then cut 1-inch-wide strips down from the center to the inner circle; do not cut along the inner circle.

7. *Tape:* Tape strips to the inside of the cone.

8. *Decorate:* Now your hat is ready to be decorated. See the ideas on page 33.

Wizard

Cover cone with fur by painting hat with glue, then wrapping the fur around it. Paint fur with glue, then sprinkle with glitter.

To make "lightning bolts," unbend paper clips, coat them with glue, then sprinkle with glitter. Insert in top of cone and secure with glue. Bend end of paper clips and hang crystals or jewels. Secure with glue.

Witchy Hat

Use shiny black poster board from an artist's supply store. "Paint" designs with glue, then sprinkle with glitter. Add black netting to the point and a feather boa to the brim, both from a fabric store.

Princess of Birdland

Cover the hat with pink fur by painting the hat with glue then covering with fur. Paint fur with glue and sprinkle with glitter.

Leafy Hat

Glue dried or cloth leaves (from a crafts store) all over the hat.

Nest and veil are made of nylon netting (from a fabric store). Get the birds, nest, and eggs at a crafts store. Collect some twigs that have fallen to the ground.

CHAPTER FOUR

Pumpkin Fever

There was a time many, many years ago in a country called Ireland when Halloween was celebrated without pumpkins. There was a simple reason for this. Pumpkins didn't grow there. But the people grew other vegetables, such as turnips, which they used for Halloween lanterns. There is an old story of that time that the Irish people tell about the origin of the jack-o'-lantern. It goes like this:

Once upon a time, there lived a man whose name was Jack. He was mean, nasty, and very, very tight-fisted with money. He grumbled every time his wife bought anything, even something as cheap as a spool of thread. He never offered to help any of the neighbors, and he refused to go to church for fear he might have to put a few pennies in the offering plate.

Late one afternoon, Jack was out walking among his apple trees. It was close to harvest time and he was checking to make sure no one was stealing his lovely ripe fruit. Suddenly the devil appeared, strolling along beside him. He's heard about me, and he's come for my soul, thought Jack. Quickly he pointed out the beautiful red apples on his trees.

"Why not help yourself to a juicy apple?" Jack offered.

The devil smacked his slippery lips and scurried to the very top of the tree, where his fiendish eyes had already picked out the very ripest fruit. Jack listened and he could hear him as he picked and munched and munched and picked. Working quickly and carefully so the devil wouldn't see him, Jack carved a cross into the bark of the tree. He knew this sign would prevent the devil from coming back down, for he could not pass over the cross.

When the devil had eaten his fill, he wiped his dribbling lips on his scraggly sleeve and began to slither down the tree. The moment he saw the cross carved into the trunk, he froze.

The Fever
(To the tune of "Fever")

It's all happening down at the patch.

Something's in the air and it's easy to catch.

It's like an itch that you can't scratch

The fever . . . pumpkin fever.

Most folks really enjoy the fuss.

Others think it is outrageous

That this thing is so contagious.

The fever . . . pumpkin fever.

It all begins with pumpkin inspecting.

Then you find you are pumpkin selecting.

And all at once you begin detecting

The fever . . . pumpkin fever.

The Colors of Halloween

Orange and black,
Orange and black,
The colors of Halloween.

Orange and black,
Orange and black,
What do these colors mean?

"I'm black," said the night.
"My darkness means fright.
Things look spooky without light."

"I'm black," said the cat.
"So am I," said the bat.
"Don't forget me," said the rat.

"I'm black too," said the hat
While on the witch's head she sat.
They all agreed and that was that.

The pumpkin, with her orange glow,
Whirled around so all would know
That she, too, should join the show.

The autumn leaves felt the same
These all were matched by fire's
  flame
From old bonfires of Celtic fame.

Orange and black
Orange and black
Halloween, Halloween!

His eyes blazed like fire and smoke poured from his nose. "You have tricked me. You are a very mean and nasty man. Help me down from this tree and I won't come back for your soul for five years," screamed the devil.

Jack caught a whiff of the devil's hot breath, tinged with the odor of moist apple skins. "If you promise *never* to come for my soul, I'll help you down," Jack replied. The devil snorted more hot breath and reluctantly agreed. Jack went immediately to work scraping the carved piece of bark from the tree trunk. As soon as the cross was removed, the devil slithered down the trunk. With a quick flick of his tail, he was gone.

Several years went by and Jack became meaner, nastier, and tighter and tighter with money. Then one day, to his wife's great relief, Jack died. Having been much too selfish to get into heaven, he was sent straight to the devil. When the devil caught sight of Jack, his eyes blazed with fire and he cried, "Get lost! You pulled a mean and nasty trick on me and I promised never to claim your soul. You can't stay here. Go back to where you came from!"

"But how will I find my way in the dark?" whined Jack. The devil tossed him a red-hot coal from the hellfire. "Put that inside the turnip you've been munching on and use that as your lantern," said the devil, gloating.

So mean, nasty, and selfish Jack was left to wander forever in lonely places with only the glow of the burning coal inside his turnip lamp to show the way. You might even see his flickering light on Halloween night . . . Mr. Jack-O'-Lantern.

That is how the Halloween jack-o'-lantern got its name. The idea to carve a face into the lantern probably originated with the ancient Celts. They used stone or wooden lanterns carved in the shape of heads to guard against evil spirits. Many, many years later it is believed that people used face lanterns on Halloween to scare away evil witches returning home from their annual meeting with the devil.

By the middle of the nineteenth century, large numbers of Irish immigrants had arrived in the United States. Among many of the traditions they brought with them was the custom of the Halloween lantern. They discovered that the pumpkin with its bright orange color, round shape, and soft insides was much better suited for this purpose than their traditional turnip. Today, everywhere in America where Halloween is celebrated, pumpkin jack-o'-lanterns are a must.

Pumpkin Face

This is it, the most important part of Halloween—it's time to transform your ordinary pumpkin into a frightening or funny jack-o'-lantern! Don't forget to save the seeds for roasting.

MATERIALS:

pumpkin

very sharp knife

large spoon

pencil and paper

1. *Study and Sketch:* Study your pumpkin carefully to find the best side and sketch a few face designs on a piece of paper.

2. *Cut and Lift:* Cut a hole around the stem, making a lid in the top of the pumpkin. (Ask an adult to help you.) Lift out the lid.

3. *Scrape:* Scrape the pulp away from the sides. Spoon out the seeds and pulp. Save the seeds for roasting.

4. *Trace and Cut:* Lightly trace your design on the pumpkin, then have an adult help you cut it.

5. *Light:* Light your pumpkin by putting a small flashlight or candle inside the pumpkin.

How to Roast Pumpkin Seeds

1. Wash the pulp from the seeds. Lay the seeds out on a towel to dry overnight.

2. Preheat oven to 350 degrees F.

3. Pour ¼ cup vegetable oil on a cookie sheet, then spread out the seeds, coating them evenly. Sprinkle lightly with salt.

4. Bake until lightly browned.

5. Cool seeds on a paper towel. Store in a covered container.

Pumpkin Head

Take time to choose a pumpkin
A giant one or small.
Carve a very frightening face
Upon this orange ball.
Put in a lighted candle,
But not before nightfall.
Then place it like a scary head
Out on the garden wall.
Or set it in the window
Or on the table in the hall.
Halloween without a pumpkin
Isn't Halloween at all!

The Legend of Sleepy Hollow

BY WASHINGTON IRVING; ADAPTED BY CARIN AND JOAN DEWHIRST

Everyone around the dinner table at Van Tassell's farm knew the story except Ichabod Crane, the new schoolmaster. Martha Gates, the town gossip, had lived in the small village of Sleepy Hollow for over eighty years, so she knew the tale very well. She told all sorts of stories but especially liked to tell those about ghosts and mysterious disappearances.

Martha's eyes brightened and her cheeks flushed as she spoke. "The gun went off with a bang and blew his noggin right off!" Her bony fist hit the table and Ichabod Crane jumped. "No time to say his last prayers, poor soldier. His head was taken clean off in a second! Buried him headless, or so the story goes. Can't say I know the spot, though, there ain't no gravestone. Poor soldier, he's probably in the old cemetery just this side of Sleepy Hollow Bridge."

Brom Bones was also at the table, and he knew the story, too. Brom, a plowman at the Van Tassell farm, was a regular guest. Brom was quite large, so farmer Van Tassell had fashioned a comfortable chair for him out of a wide tree stump. Brom came to the Van Tassell farm to work but also to visit the fair Katrina, farmer Van Tassell's daughter.

The guests listened as they always did when old Martha told her tales to newcomers at Sleepy Hollow. They enjoyed watching the strangers' reactions. Ichabod Crane grew pale as he listened. He felt uneasy and kept shifting his long skinny legs nervously.

Several things bothered Ichabod besides the story. He was the new schoolmaster in town, and he liked knowing more than anyone else. He had no patience for local legends, unless he was telling them. And Ichabod didn't like ghost stories, for his imagination made too much of them. As Martha's story progressed, he dreaded walking home alone more and more. If there was a way to avoid passing the old cemetery, he wanted to.

Brom Bones also bothered Ichabod. "He's the strongest man in these parts and can ride like the wind," farmer Van Tassell had said. Brom had a loud laugh that irritated Ichabod, but the way Brom looked at Katrina, Ichabod's favorite pupil, upset him more. Lately Ichabod couldn't look at Katrina without blushing and coughing nervously. Brom Bones never seemed nervous, just strong, calm, and confident.

Martha continued her story. "Poor soldier, his soul won't rest. They say he rises from his grave at midnight and whistles for his horse. He rides and rides till dawn, carrying his head at his side. Could be he's looking for someone to run down. Maybe he wants to steal a new head for himself! Mind you, he stays this side of Sleepy Hollow Bridge, but mark my words, be careful on the road after midnight and keep a—"

Farmer Van Tassell stopped Martha midsentence. "Now, Martha, you'll frighten our friend Mr. Crane. Look at his face. He's the color of milk. Don't you worry, Mr. Crane. Martha's tale is older than she is and probably hogwash. Isn't that right, Brom?"

"Can't say I know which of them old tales is true and which is not." Brom winked at Katrina. He glanced over at a chalk-faced Ichabod and added, "Better give our new school-master your fastest horse, Van Tassell. He don't look fit to walk home tonight." Brom bellowed a low, deep laugh, "And if it ain't past midnight to boot!"

A few minutes later, Ichabod bid everyone good night and walked to the barn with farmer Van Tassell. He looked back at the farmhouse. Through the window he saw Mrs. Van Tassell and Katrina help Brom on with his long black cape. Ichabod thought Katrina was radiant in the amber lamplight. Her wild red-brown hair was like a deep golden halo, and as she pushed it away from her face with a delicate hand, he could see that she was blushing. That tiresome Brom is probably teasing her again, thought Ichabod. He watched Katrina curtsy and smile as Brom bowed to her and the other guests.

Farmer Van Tassell saddled up old Buck, handed Ichabod a slender switch, and sent him on his way. Before long Ichabod lost sight of the warm glow of the farmhouse. There were no street lanterns, the path was lit only by the white light of the full moon. As Ichabod followed the dirt road deeper and deeper into the woods, the tall trees now and then blocked out the moon. The shadows of tree branches looked to Ichabod like extended bony arms with clawlike hands. He winced occasionally because he could almost feel the shadows scrape his head and body as he rode beneath the trees.

A sharp, bitter wind had come up an hour before, and it was now blowing fiercely. Ichabod pulled his woolen coat closer to him, trying to keep the cold—and the fear—from creeping into his bones. I shall enjoy this midnight ride, he thought without conviction, and that rustling is just the normal noise of the wind in the trees, nothing to worry about.

Ichabod looked up into the trees and noticed how silvery the leaves looked when the moonlight shone on their undersides. A brown hoot owl took flight and with a "Whoooooo-whoo-whooot!" swooped close to Ichabod's head on its way to a new perch. Ichabod gasped and quickly leaned down out of the way. His beaklike nose bumped against Buck's stiff mane and he grimaced in pain. The impact jostled his glasses, and though he extended an awkward arm to catch them, they fell to the ground. Ichabod heard the high, light sound of breaking glass as Buck's hind hoof crushed the spectacles.

The noise spooked Buck, and he reared. Ichabod jerked back painfully and was almost thrown from the saddle. He pulled madly at the reins and tried to yell "whoa!" but panic tightened his throat. His heart and Buck's hooves pounded harder and harder and faster and faster. Ichabod closed his eyes and strained forward in the saddle. He leaned so close to Buck's head that he could hear the steed's desperate panting.

Moments later Ichabod dared to open his eyes a sliver. After squinting and blinking, he was certain that he could see the iron gates of the old cemetery ahead—although without his glasses everything was blurred. Ghosts seemed to dance lightly on the gravestones. "Ah, it's only the fog rising over the resting dead souls," Ichabod comforted himself. Then he heard a long, piercing whistle. He thought it was his own breathing, until he heard it again.

Next, Ichabod heard a horse coming up from behind. He turned and saw in the distance a dark figure sitting tall and broad on the back of a massive black stallion. Buck was no match for the great horse, but Ichabod gave him the switch anyway.

What have I to be afraid of? thought Ichabod. It's probably just someone else on his way home. He turned back again to get a better look. Ichabod froze. He squinted and blinked and didn't want to believe his eyes, but the moon clearly shone on a headless rider!

Ichabod thought his heart would stop. He whipped Buck on and dug his heels into the horse's sides. He was practically standing in the stirrups now, crying plaintively in

Buck's ear, "Giddy-up, Buck. Faster! Faster! Faster!" Ichabod thought he could see Sleepy Hollow Bridge up ahead, but couldn't completely trust his hazy vision.

Then the black horse and the terrifying rider were beside him. The stallion's eyes gleamed like polished onyx and frothy sweat dripped down his shiny, sinewy neck. Ichabod saw the rider stand in the stirrups. His full black cape rose behind him like black wings. He lifted a round object high above his shoulders—was it a severed head?

The rider was poised ready to toss it—but for what seemed like an eternity all Ichabod knew was the synchronized galloping of Buck and the black stallion and the thumping within his chest. Finally, Ichabod could stand it no longer and turned away. The round object smashed against Ichabod's back, knocking his body from the horse and the breath from his lungs. He rolled into the dirt and weeds by the side of the road.

The next morning a young man returned Buck to the Van Tassell farm. "Found him by Sleepy Hollow Bridge," he said. "Caught him while he munched on some weeds. Must say I was surprised to see a busted pumpkin nearby—still wonder where that came from." Farmer Van Tassell asked his neighbors about Ichabod Crane. No one had seen him, so the farmer went to Sleepy Hollow Bridge to look for clues. He found the smashed pumpkin and deep hoof marks in the dirt. Van Tassell followed the tracks back into the woods and found a pair of broken glasses. "Why, these look just like Mr. Crane's," he remarked to himself. He formed a search party, but they never found a body.

Brom Bones married Katrina Van Tassell that following spring, just as everyone had expected. Ichabod Crane did not attend. At the wedding someone asked Brom Bones about the disappearance of the schoolmaster. "They say the headless horseman got him," Brom Bones turned to Katrina and winked, "but I guess we'll never know for sure."

Pumpkin Head Cupcakes

Carving faces into pumpkins is great fun, but frosting cupcakes so they look like little pumpkin heads is *sweeter* fun! Instead of spreading frosting with a knife, put a small amount of frosting in a plastic bag, then squeeze it onto the cupcakes.

INGREDIENTS FOR 8 TO 10 CUPCAKES:

2 eggs, at room temperature

3/4 cup honey

6 tablespoons butter or margarine, softened

1/2 cup plain yogurt

2/3 cup canned pumpkin

2 cups unbleached white flour

1 teaspoon baking soda

1 teaspoon ginger

1/2 teaspoon cinnamon

1/2 teaspoon nutmeg

1/2 teaspoon allspice

1/4 teaspoon cardamom

8 to 10 green gumdrops

FROSTING INGREDIENTS:

4 ounces cream cheese, softened

1 stick butter, softened

3 3/4 cups powdered sugar

1 teaspoon vanilla extract

orange, red, and green food coloring

1 teaspoon (or so) milk

1. Preheat oven to 350 degrees F.

2. Using an electric mixer, beat the eggs in a large bowl until they are frothy.

3. Add the honey, butter, yogurt, pumpkin, flour, baking soda, ginger, cinnamon, nutmeg, allspice, and cardamom, and beat at medium speed until well mixed (about two minutes). Batter will be rather thick.

4. Place paper liners in muffin tin. Fill lined muffin cups to top with batter.

5. Bake for 35 to 40 minutes or until muffins are slightly golden on the top. While cupcakes cool, make the frosting.

6. In a medium-sized bowl, beat cream cheese, butter, sugar, and vanilla extract together until smooth.

Brown frosting: Spoon ¼ of frosting mixture into a small bowl and add equal drops of red and green food coloring to make dark brown. Mix until color is smooth and uniform.

Orange frosting: To remaining frosting add 10 to 15 drops of orange food coloring and beat again. Add more or less food coloring depending on the color you prefer. If frosting is too thick to spread, add one teaspoon or so of milk and beat again.

7. Spoon a small amount of orange frosting into one corner of a plastic bag. Snip ¼ inch off the end and squeeze bag until frosting comes out. On a piece of waxed paper, practice making dots and lines of frosting. Beginning at the top of one cupcake, make lines of orange frosting as shown.

8. Place a small amount of brown frosting in another bag and snip one end. Make eyes, nose, and mouth, then add a green gum drop as the stem.

Pumpkins are cultivated in most parts of North America and in other parts of the world. A trip to the local pumpkin patch to choose the perfect specimen for a jack-o'-lantern has become a special part of the celebration of Halloween.

According to the 1992 <u>Guinness Book of World Records</u>, a pumpkin weighing 827 pounds was grown in Puyallup, Washington, by Joel Holland in 1991. It measured 14 feet in circumference.

"Jack-o'-lantern" is also a term given to the strange, flickering light that frequently shines at night over swampy marshlands. It is believed that this light is caused by spontaneous combustion of the gases escaping from rotting stumps and logs.

CHAPTER FIVE

Trick or Treat

Trick-or-treat . . . the perfect game for mischievous Halloween! Troops of masqueraders in countless disguises join together in a masked threat to play friendly tricks if not given proper treats. The custom of going from door to door begging for candy, nuts, apples, and pennies while dressed in outlandish costume has become the most popular event of Halloween. This tradition, as we know it today, probably has its beginnings centuries ago in other celebrations in other places.

Begging was part of a Celtic celebration in ancient Ireland. On October 31, peasants would form a long procession and go from farmhouse to farmhouse asking for donations in honor of Muck Olla (muck-oh-LAH), a pagan god. The parade leader wore a white robe and a mask in the shape of a horse's head. He would deliver warnings about what misfortunes might occur if Muck Olla was not treated properly. Hoping to ensure the good fortune of their crops and animals, farmers gladly donated potatoes, corn, butter, eggs, and even gold coins.

Begging was also part of an old custom in England called "a souling." On All Souls' Day (November 2), people dressed up and paraded along the streets singing a song. In exchange for special square-shaped currant buns, or "soul-cakes," the beggars promised to say extra prayers for the dead souls of the donor's loved ones. Sometimes the soulers carried the skull of a horse attached to a pole. This was known as the "hodening horse" and was believed to bring good fortune to all who gave generously.

Trick-Treating

Come along trick-treating with me
Choose whatever you want to be!
Be a pirate, be a tiger
Be a princess, be a spider
Be a monster, be a bat
Be a ghost, be a cat
Be a dancer, be a dragon
Be a gypsy, be a phantom
Be a werewolf, be a corpse
Be a cowboy, be a horse
Be a witch, be a wizard
Be an owl, be a lizard
Be a clown, be a vampire
Be a bride, be an umpire
Be a bee, be an elf
Be anything . . . except <u>yourself</u>!

Halloween Night
(To the tune of "A-Hunting We Will Go")

A-haunting we will go

A-haunting we will go

With masks on our faces we'll go lots of places

And frighten folks we know.

A-tricking we will go

A-tricking we will go

We'll trick-or-treat for things to eat

As house to house we go.

Masquerade

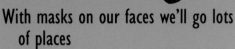

Masquerade . . .

Behind the mask you're not afraid.

Masquerade . . .

Your dream identity is made.

Masquerade . . .

A trick-or-treating escapade.

Masquerade . . .

The best game you've ever played.

A Halloween Riddle

First they dress in green,

Then they change to brown;

And some will even wear

A red or golden gown.

What are they?

(leaves)

Through the years this custom changed. Children became the principal beggars on All Souls' Day. Their chant has remained as a rhyme in literature even though the custom has long since died:

> Soul, soul! For a soul cake!
> I pray, good mistress, for a soul cake!
> An apple or a pear, or a plum or a cherry.
> Any good thing to make us merry.
> One for Peter, two for Paul,
> Three for Him who made us all.
> Up with the kettle and down with the pan.
> Give us good alms and we'll be gone.

Tricking has probably always been a part of Halloween, too. In early times people feared the evil tricks witches might play as they returned from their secret sabbats on October 31. In parts of Europe there was an old belief that fairies and goblins roamed about on Halloween night causing all sorts of trouble, such as spilled milk and curdled cream. Lots of practical jokes were blamed on these little creatures.

In some parts of America, the night before Halloween was called "Mischief Night" and serious mischief was carried out. The next morning people found house numbers and street signs changed; gates were gone and farm animals had wandered off; lawn furniture was discovered in trees or on roofs. Today the tricking is kept to the strictly harmless.

When one is up to mischief, disguise is a wise precaution. Wearing masks and costumes to disguise or change one's identity is a tradition with a very long history and was a part of most of the very oldest cultures. Early peoples used disguises to frighten away or charm evil spirits. The ancient Celts wore costumes of animal heads and skins. These disguises were a way of hiding from the scary and powerful spirits of the dead that they believed were free to roam the earth on that particular night.

Much of the excitement of Halloween lies in the selection of the perfect costume. Once a year, you have a chance to become whatever you want. And it is the one and only night that you can roam neighborhood streets in your secret disguise and collect sweet treasures. Delicious fantasy . . . the special allure of Halloween!

Sweet Fruit Dips

If you like caramel apples, you'll love caramel apple slices. With this recipe you can indulge all your creative cravings—dried apricots dipped in white chocolate, banana chips covered with caramel, strawberries dipped in smooth dark chocolate. Invent your own combinations; surprise your friends.

INGREDIENTS FOR DIPS:

16-ounce package chocolate chips

1 tablespoon plus 1 teaspoon butter

1 cup white chocolate chips

1 cup caramels

Fruit Suggestions (choose 2 or 3):

Fresh: Apples, strawberries, bananas, grapes

Dried: Apricots, banana chips

The Celts and the Romans probably made apples part of Halloween traditions. Bobbing for apples is still a popular game at Halloween parties. It comes from the Celtic belief in the Island of Apples—where all sorts of fruits grew magically. To get to this enchanted isle, one had to pass through water.

Nuts (choose one):

1/2 cup chopped almonds

1/2 cup chopped walnuts

1. Prepare each of the dipping sauces in a double boiler over low heat. Melt the dark chocolate and butter together, but melt the white chocolate bits and the caramels by themselves.

2. Cover a cookie sheet with waxed paper; secure with tape.

3. Slice bananas and spear with a toothpick. Cut apples into slices.

4. Dip each piece of fruit in desired topping. Do not cover pieces completely, except bananas. Sprinkle fruits with chopped nuts if desired.

5. Place on cookie sheet until coating hardens.

Halloween Treats

Gumdrops, lollipops, chocolate galore,

Caramels and candy all over the floor.

Bubble gum, jellybeans, pennies, and fruit.

Halloween fun is counting the loot.

The New Girl

It was an unusually wet and hazy Halloween. Even the air was not like Halloween—it was not crisp and wild. Late in the afternoon, the fog had moved in quickly and seemed to devour the seaside town. Now after sunset, a thick, still mist covered everything. On this curious Halloween night, as Annie Boyle and her parents drove to Julie's party, they met the new girl.

Annie saw her first, when the car's headlights shone on a small figure walking just a few feet ahead. "Dad, it looks like Alison," she said. "Please stop so we can give her a ride." They pulled up behind the girl.

The girl was dressed as a bobby-soxer—a teenager in the fifties. Her clothes were obviously authentic, probably hand-me-downs from her mother. She wore a faded blue dress covered with an old-fashioned daisy print. The full, gathered skirt came to just below her knees. She'd knotted a matching polka-dot scarf at her neck, and a charm bracelet dangled loosely around her wrist. Although she was Annie's age, about thirteen, her short blue socks and brown-and-white saddle shoes made her look younger.

Annie lowered her window and called out, "Alison!" The young girl turned toward the car and Annie's mother gasped. The face was not Alison's. This new face, which Mrs. Boyle had never seen before, was deathly pale.

Annie spoke to the new girl. "Oh, sorry, we thought you were Alison on her way to Julie's party."

"I am on my way to the party," the girl said softly.

"Why don't you ride with us?" Annie's mother made the offer, but felt troubled. She quickly added, "It's too dark and foggy to walk by yourself." The new girl climbed into the car and said her name was Sara. She and Annie talked about their costumes, parties, and trick-or-treating. Annie listed all the people who would be at Julie's party, and Sara listened attentively, as if for names she knew. By the time they got to Julie's house, Annie had made a new friend.

The front door of Julie's house was wide open in expectation of party guests. Through the open doorway, the Boyles and Sara could see a variety of monsters, witches, ghosts, and mummies milling about inside. Mr. and Mrs. Boyle followed Annie and Sara up a walkway lined with grinning, glowing pumpkins. Julie's mother, Mrs. Miles, greeted them with a booming voice.

"It's the Boyles! Oh, Annie, look at you! You are the perfect cheerleader. Now who is this bobby-soxer?" Mrs. Miles turned to Sara.

Mrs. Boyle spoke, "This is Sara. She was walking here so we—"

Mrs. Miles interrupted to call her husband a few feet away. "Fred! Come and see the cheerleader and the bobby-soxer, you'll love them."

Sara and Annie twirled slowly as Mr. and Mrs. Miles admired Sara's outfit. "How I loved the sound my charm bracelet made whenever I moved my arm." Mrs. Miles took Sara's wrist to examine her charm bracelet. "My dear, your hands are like ice! We must get you a sweater before you go out. You can't go outside with short sleeves. You'll catch your death!"

"I've got just the thing for her," said Mr. Miles and went to find Sara a sweater. It was beige and bulky and had a huge letter B sewn on one pocket. "This is my old letterman's sweater from college. It's my prized possession, so take good care of it."

The large costumed group was finally ready to go trick-or-treating. As they walked through the streets, trailed by the adults, houses appeared suddenly through the fog. After stopping at several homes, Annie whispered in Sara's ear, "The next house is haunted—it's the undertaker's. The ghosts of all the people who he's put in coffins live in his attic. It's the big house across the street with all the windows."

Annie gestured to a large house with a tall, steep roof and a deep porch. The owners had taken time to give their house an extra-haunted Halloween feeling. Through the fog, candles burned in each window. Wisps of mist had settled on the lush lawn, where carved pumpkins glared and snarled at the trick-or-treaters. Right below the sharp, pointed rooftop, the girls could see a small circular window where a dim lantern glowed and flickered. As the group approached the door, they felt cobwebs brush their faces.

Someone rang the doorbell, and it resonated deep inside the house. The door opened with a rusty, heavy creak. An older woman stepped forward holding a platter heaped with colorful candy. "Trick or treat!" sang the group, and the woman's eyes twinkled. "Hello, my pretties, happy Halloween! Now, what have we here?" Her eyes surveyed the group, and she gasped or laughed at ghouls, ghosts, and clowns. The undertaker appeared behind her. He wore a comfortable sweater, carried a paper, and had a pipe clenched between his teeth. He surveyed the disguised crowd, but when he saw Sara his mouth dropped open and his pipe clattered to the floor. His wife turned and jumped. The undertaker's face had gone pale.

"Is that you, Sara?" he whispered.

Sara moved quickly away from the door, bumping into Annie as she ran off the porch. Annie followed her and soon both girls were enveloped by the fog.

The undertaker turned to his wife. "I've seen that young girl before," he said. "It was a long, long time ago—almost forty years, yes, forty years ago today. I've never forgotten that face . . . ."

"Now, James, you stop this nonsense. That girl was in costume and just reminded you of someone else. Under all that gruesome white makeup, she could have been anyone."

"I don't believe that was makeup, and she wasn't in costume." He gave his wife a serious, warning look, and they closed the door.

Halfway down the next block, Annie was trying to catch up to Sara, who was still running. "Sara, slow down! Please, I'm out of breath." Sara stopped and Annie caught up with her. "I've never seen anyone run like you did, and you're not even out of breath! What's wrong?"

"Please, Annie, I want to go home. Can your father drive me?"

"Well, sure, but it was just getting fun and—"

"I want to go; I have to go home *now*!" Sara pleaded.

Annie could just barely see her father and the other parents standing at the end of the block. "Did you like the haunted house?" Mr. Boyle asked with a chuckle as the two girls approached.

"Sara didn't like it at all and now she wants to go home," said Annie.

Sara looked cold and frightened, so Mr. Boyle quickly walked her to his car. "Annie, go back and join the gang. I'll come back for you and mom later."

Sara directed Mr. Boyle out of town. When they got to a rusty, broken mailbox at the end of a dirt road, she told him to stop. "I'll walk from here," she said. "The road is too narrow and bumpy for your car."

"No, I'll walk you to . . ." At that moment Mr. Boyle heard a deep, angry barking. His headlights caught the glaring eyes of a snarling dog.

"That's my dog, Boxer. He'll take care of me until I get in the house," said Sara. She got out of the car, and the dog ran to her and wagged its tail. Mr. Boyle started to get out of the car, but the dog bared its teeth and lunged at him. Sara waved him back in and

called to the dog. They ran off toward a broken-down cabin with a single light burning in the window. Mr. Boyle watched them until he thought Sara and Boxer had reached the house.

The fog lifted during the night and the next morning was bright and crisp. Mr. Miles called the Boyles, worried about his prized sweater. "We let Sara wear it home," explained Mr. Boyle. "But don't worry, we'll go by and get it right now."

When Annie and Mr. Boyle got to the dirt driveway, there was no sign of Boxer. Mr. Boyle was relieved. Annie and her father walked to the weather-beaten cabin and knocked on the door several times. An old, hunched woman came to the door.

"Are you Sara's mother?" Annie asked brightly.

The old woman looked surprised. "Well, yes, I guess I still would be her mother, but . . ."

"Is Sara here? We need the sweater we lent her last night. It's Mr. Miles's and he wants it back," said Annie.

"You lent my Sara a sweater? I don't think so." The woman began to close the door.

Mr. Boyle spoke up. "We're sorry to bother you, but your daughter came out trick-or-treating with us last night. She was wearing a blue dress, saddle shoes, and bobby socks."

The old woman opened the door wide again, "Did you say bobby socks and a blue dress?"

"Yes, and a blue scarf with polka dots," said Annie.

The old woman looked at Annie and her father, then gazed into the distance. "So she's out and about again. . . . Guess it was forty years ago last night since the accident . . . you're not the first to see her."

"What accident, what do you mean?" demanded Mr. Boyle.

"I mean that my little one's been dead for forty years now. She and her dog, Boxer, died together. It was a terrible accident on a foggy Halloween night. They were . . ." The old woman lost her voice as her eyes swam with tears. After a moment, she spoke again. "She's buried in town beneath a sweet marble angel." The woman lifted a corner of her apron to wipe her eyes.

Annie and her father didn't talk as they drove back to town. They were both thinking about Sara, the mysterious accident, the party the night before, and the sweater. On a whim, Mr. Boyle decided not to drive directly to Mr. Miles's, but to stop and go to the cemetery instead.

Annie got out of the car first and ran to the far end of the graveyard, not sure exactly where she was going. When Mr. Boyle found her, she was standing by a grave with a small marble angel on its headstone. She didn't look up when her father touched her shoulder. She was mesmerized, for there was Mr. Miles's sweater folded neatly at the angel's feet.

Tricky Treat Bag

This bag is tricky because it glows in the dark—but it's super simple to make! Use luminous paints and carry a small flashlight—when the bag stops glowing, reactivate it with your flashlight. After Halloween, use this bag to carry your books to school. That way, every day will be as much fun as Halloween!

MATERIALS:

canvas bag

fabric marker

luminous and regular fabric paint

canvas in various colors

plastic jewels

STEPS:

1. *Sketch and Paint:* Copy one of our designs or create your own. Halloween books usually have super-scary pictures you can use for inspiration. Sketch design first onto the bag with fabric marker. Paint over the sketch.

2. *Paint Again:* Outline your design with luminous paint.

3. *Decorate:* Here are some ideas on how to decorate your bag.

Planet Bag

Cut a moon, stars, and planets out of canvas and glue onto bag. Outline with fabric paint.

Glue on jewels from a craft store and apply fabric paint to edges.

Graveyard Bag

Imagine a spooky graveyard scene with ghosts and gravestones and sketch it onto the bag.

MAKE TRICK-OR-TREATING SAFE:

• NEVER TRICK-OR-TREAT ALONE! Go with a group.
• Put reflective tape on your costume to reflect headlights.
• Carry a flashlight to light up curbs, steps, and potholes.
• If it is chilly, dress warmly underneath your costume.
• Examine all treats carefully before eating.
• Playful tricks can be fun. Serious mischief can be very
   dangerous. Be a responsible Halloween player!

CHAPTER SIX

Wily Wee Folk

Halloween is magical. For the ancient Celtic peoples of Ireland, Scotland, and Wales, scary ghosts and evil monsters emerged from the underworld on this celebrated evening. Spirits with magical powers also came out of their hiding places in deep caves and under huge rocks. These spirits appeared in many sizes, shapes, and costumes and went by as many names—fairies, elves, goblins, brownies, trolls, and leprechauns. They shared one common quality—all of them were famous for their wily ways. Crafty, sly, and clever, they could trick folks quicker than you can blink.

Some groups of wee folk were especially fond of music and lively dancing. The Celts in Wales believed that on Halloween certain fairy music possessed unusual powers. This story is still being told there:

Once upon a time there was a hardworking farmer who lived with his patient wife and devoted dog on a plot of land way, way out in the country. The farmer worked hard in the fields during the day, but at night he enjoyed playing his fiddle. He loved music and he loved to play for folks to dance. Every night his companionable wife danced and danced while the dog watched and wagged his tail in time with the tunes. After many years of this nightly routine, the wife began to tire and the dog's tail began to lose its rhythm. The farmer decided it was time to find a larger audience. The next evening, the fiddling farmer packed his fiddle on his back and he and the dog set out, each seeking new territory. As luck would have it, this particular evening was Halloween.

The two pals walked for several miles, the dog especially enjoying the autumn-scented air. Suddenly he stopped, his ears stood straight up, and his tail began wagging. Then the farmer's ears heard the notes as well. The music seemed to be coming from inside a dense thicket, and a tiny light shined out from the underbrush. The two companions wandered closer

The Child and the Fairies

The woods are full of fairies!
The trees are all alive;
The river overflows with them,
See how they dip and dive!
What funny little fellows!
What dainty little dears!
They dance and leap, and prance and peep,
And utter fairy cheers!

I'd Like to Tame a Fairy

I'd like to tame a fairy,
To keep it on a shelf,
To see it wash its little face,
And dress its little self.
I'd teach it pretty manners,
It always should say "Please;"
And then you know I'd make it sew,
And curtsy with its knees!

Pooka Polka

(To the tune of "The Hokey Pokey")

Gather your friends in a circle and describe what a monster Pooka is like. Have everyone join in the actions. For the Polka parts do a step-step-step-kick. Start by putting the right foot down, then the left foot, now the right foot, and then kicking with the left. Repeat this while turning around in place.

Kick my right foot in

Kick my right foot out

Kick my right foot in and shake it all about

Do the Pooka Polka and turn myself around

That's what it's all about.

REFRAIN:

Do the Pooka Polka, do the Pooka Polka, do the Pooka Polka

That's what it's all about. **(Clap hands.)**

Kick my left foot in

Kick my left foot out

Kick my left foot in and shake it all about

Do the Pooka Polka and turn myself about

That's what it's all about.

(Repeat refrain after each action sequence.)

Put my hairy arms in . . .

Put my bushy head in . . .

Put my scary face in . . .

Put my monster self in . . .

and found themselves at the entrance to a deep cave filled with curious little people, some playing instruments and others dancing with great gaiety.

The dog's coat bristled and his ears shot backward. With his tail limp between his legs, he hit the trail for home. The farmer, however, could not resist going inside. When his eyes adjusted to the light he observed the tiny folks dressed from chin to toe in dark, tightly knit garments. They all wore short, forest-green vests, each with two large silver buttons. They were dancing joyously in a large circle.

Suddenly it hit the farmer—this was a fairy ring! A bolt of fear went through him for he knew that once he stepped inside that ring he would never be able to leave. He turned to get away but as he did so, all the fairy faces turned toward him. The compelling stare in that circle of eyes took the run out of his legs, and soon he could do nothing but stay and fiddle with the fairies.

The next morning the worried wife went in search of her husband. The dog led her back to the same dense thicket, but the air was quiet. He sniffed and sniffed in search of the cave entrance but without luck.

The wife and the dog were alone the entire year until the next Halloween, when the dog yearned for another walk, and the two set out. Once again they found themselves near the same dense thicket. The dog's ears stood up and his tail began wagging. The wife heard the sounds, too, and her heart stopped. She followed the music to the cave entrance and looked inside. There were the tiny folk in their forest-green vests dancing wildly, and in the center of the ring was her husband, fiddling his heart out. And he still is to this very day. People say you can catch a glimpse of him. But only on Halloween.

There is a very large, very old, and very famous underground cave in Ireland that you can visit anytime called Brugh (broo) of the Boyne (boin). It is said to have been home to the King of the Tuatha Dé Danann (too-AH-ha da dan-ANN), a race of heroic warriors who lived in Ireland many years before the Celts. According to the earliest Irish folklore, the Tuatha Dé Danann were great fighters and fought battles valiantly, but they were defeated by fierce invaders. The Tuatha Dé Danann were forced by their captors to live underground. Many years later they emerged as small men with unusual powers. These tiny creatures became the leprechauns and other wily wee folk of Irish myths. Are these tiny people real and do they exist today? Most people aren't brave enough to deny that they do, especially on Halloween!

Pot O'Gold Gorp

"**G**orp" is another name for trail mix or just simply a quick-energy snack. It consists of a healthy conglomeration of whole toasted grains, nuts, and dried fruits that is delicious, nutritious, and fun to eat. This recipe has a Halloween flavor with the addition of toasted pumpkin seeds. It has a Halloween "treat," too, with the addition of just a few candy M & Ms . . . a wee touch of gold from a generous leprechaun.

**INGREDIENTS FOR
4-1/2 MAGIC CUPFULS:**

1/2 cup pumpkin seeds

1 tablespoon vegetable oil

1/4 teaspoon salt

1/2 cup shredded coconut

1 cup rolled oats

1/3 cup slivered almonds

1/3 cup sesame seeds

1/3 cup sunflower seeds

1/4 cup brown sugar

*1/4 cup "gold" (yellow)
candy-coated chocolates
or M&Ms*

*1/4 cup each of dried dates,
apples, apricots, figs,
currants (sour cherries
and cranberries, if
available)*

1. Save the seeds from pumpkin carving. Wash off the pulp, then spread the seeds on paper towels to dry overnight. Shake into a mixing bowl and toss with vegetable oil. Place on a cookie sheet, sprinkle with salt, and bake 15 minutes at 350 degrees F.

2. Spread shredded coconut on a baking sheet. Bake at 250 degrees F until golden brown, 15 to 20 minutes.

3. Lightly roast the oats and nuts in a heavy pan on the stove over medium heat, stirring constantly for 5 minutes.

4. Add the seeds to the oatnut mixture. Continue cooking and stirring for 10 minutes.

5. Sprinkle with sugar and salt, cooking until the brown sugar melts. Remove from heat.

6. When mixture is cool, add the coconut, "gold," and dried fruit. Store in airtight container.

Some people believed that goblins could be bribed with food to do tasks around the house, but they were full of mischief as well. It was thought that goblins stole little babies and left tiny goblins ("changelings") in their place. Mothers had to trick the goblins to return their children.

Some Irish lore depicts the Pooka as a supernatural being who goes about on Halloween ruining all unpicked fruit.

The Return of the Leprechaun

Michael O'Shaunessy knew all about leprechauns. His grandfather had lived out in the country near Tipperary in the old days and had actually seen one. Michael had heard the story many times but he never tired of hearing it again.

"Michael, my boy," said Grandpa O'Shaunessy, "you don't see a leprechaun first, you hear him. Leprechauns are shoemakers and they are always busy making shoes for fairies. If ever you're out for a stroll in the late afternoon, listen for a tap-tap-tap. That'll be the leprechaun's hammer working away."

"But, Grandpa, tell me again what they look like," Michael pleaded.

"Mikey, me lad," said Grandpa O'Shaunessy with a grin, "there's no mistaking a leprechaun for any other fairy. He is a small fellow with red hair, twinkling black eyes, and a large mischievous grin. He wears a long green coat with big silver buttons and trousers that only come to his knees. He has white stockings and shoes with shiny silver buckles. And of course, a cobbler's apron made of leather."

"Grandpa Tom, what do they sound like when they talk?" asked Michael. This was his favorite question. He knew his grandfather would tell the whole story now.

"Oh, begorrah," chuckled his grandpa. "Once you've heard a leprechaun's voice, you never forget it. Seems like yesterday that I was walking into Tipperary and I surprised the little fellow hammering away in the ditch alongside the road. I jumped down beside him and grabbed hold of the back of his small green coat. He was furious and demanded that I let him go in this high-pitched, squeaky voice that pierced my ears like the thorn from a rose. I told him I wouldn't let go until he took me to where he had hidden his pot of gold. He screamed and squirmed and then he reached into his pocket and pulled out a box of snuff. He took a pinch and flung it in my face. I sneezed and he disappeared."

"But, Grandpa, where does a leprechaun get all his gold?" asked Michael. For months he had been hoarding his allowance and the money he made from his paper route in order to buy a bicycle. A pot of gold sounded like a dream come true.

"Oh, laddy, don't you know the leprechauns are very, very old people and they keep every single penny they get. My little man was probably three hundred years old. In that many years he would have saved up quite an enormous treasure. I regret to this day that I didn't grab his arms and hold him tighter so he couldn't have reached into his pocket. He was quick with the snuff . . . it was fairy dust, you know. It is very powerful stuff."

"But couldn't you have gone back in a day or two and grabbed him again?" asked Michael. "Don't leprechauns live in the same place for a long time?"

"Oh to be sure, Mikey, I walked by that ditch on my way to town for years and years after that. I listened and listened for the tap-tap-tap, but I never heard it again. The little chap probably figured I wouldn't be so easily fooled the next time. And rightly so! I'm sure he dug up his treasure and moved far, far away from Tipperary."

"Grandpa Tom, can you tell me where exactly the ditch was?" asked Michael. In all the years he had listened to the leprechaun story, he had never asked that question. But now he wanted that bicycle. A pot of gold would make it so easy!

"Mikey, my lad, if you're thinking of finding that ditch, don't bother yourself. There's a house on the property now. The ditch is all filled in and they built a fence on top of it. Old Mrs. McClary lives there . . . you know, your mother's friend who has all the beautiful flowers. But, tell me now, is it the gold you've set your mind on?" The old man sensed a change of direction in Michael's line of questioning.

Michael hesitated a minute and then nodded his head and confessed, "If I had the leprechaun's gold, I could buy a new bicycle right away. If I have to wait until I save my own money, it could take almost a year!"

Grandpa Tom sighed and muttered to himself, "Oh, will the wee ones never learn? Young man, if you're smart you'll listen closely. No one ever outsmarts a leprechaun. These little men have spent more years than you and I can count tricking folks like us. My father and even my grandfather thought they could get their hands on that golden treasure. No such luck! Each time, the leprechaun distracted them with clever talk and then he was gone. Yes siree, even your own father tried for the gold."

Michael gasped in astonishment, "Dad actually met up with a leprechaun? Why hasn't he told me about it?"

"Too embarrassed to admit being fooled, I suppose," said Grandpa Tom. "He never gave me the details, either, just that he had missed a chance to get rich quick. Take my advice and save up your own pot of gold. But you'd better run along now. You've wasted too much time talking about leprechauns!"

Michael hugged his grandpa and started on the road for home. He tried, but he couldn't put the thoughts out of his mind. His own father, his Grandpa Tom, his great-grandfather, and his great-great-grandfather *all* had been tricked by leprechauns! It was high time someone collected a pot of gold.

He realized it would only be a little bit out of his way to go by Mrs. McClary's place. After all it was late afternoon and Grandpa even said that was the perfect time to listen for leprechauns. As he turned the corner he spotted the McClary house with its neat white fence surrounding the beautiful flower garden. When Michael first heard the sound, he thought it was a woodpecker. But . . . there it was again. Tap-tap-tap! Michael's heart began to pound to the same beat. He walked softly over to the fence and bent down to peek between the clumps of blooming foxgloves. There he was . . . the tiniest little man Michael had ever seen! His back was turned as he hammered away at his work. Michael carefully leaned over the fence, reached down through the thick flowers, and grabbed the leprechaun firmly with both hands. He pulled him straight up and held him in front of his face, pinning the leprechaun's arms tight against his little green coat. "I've got you now and you're not going to fool me!" cried Michael, his face flushed with excitement.

"And who might I be trying to fool who is nearly squeezing the life's breath out of me?" squeaked the leprechaun.

"I'm Michael O'Shaunessy and I'm not going to stop squeezing until you show me where your pot of gold is buried," said Michael in his firmest and most serious voice.

"Your grip speaks loudly for your determination, my lad. Say now, are you any relation to Tom O' Shaunessy? I met up with him awhile back. Chap about your age. Too bad about his allergy to fairy dust." The leprechaun spoke rapidly and his eyes twinkled.

"So you are the very same leprechaun that tricked my grandfather," cried Michael. And he clutched the little man so tightly he nearly popped the buttons off his tiny coat. "Take me to your gold, and no tricks this time!"

Having no other choice, the leprechaun directed Michael down the road a mile or so out of Tipperary. It seemed a long, long way to Michael and after a while they ran out of farmhouses. The leprechaun suddenly shouted, "Say, laddy, take a look over yonder hill. The sunset is so blazing it looks like a fire!"

"Keep gazing at it yourself," answered Michael, tightening his grip on the little man. "I'm not taking my eyes off you until you show me your treasure. Hurry it up!"

The leprechaun did not speak again until they came to a huge open field full of ragweed. He pointed to a large plant and said, "Now if you dig under this ragweed you'll find a great supply of gold . . . enough to buy whatever you want."

Michael beamed with satisfaction as he thought about the shiny new bicycle. It would soon be his! He released his grip on the leprechaun and watched as the tiny fellow scurried out of sight down a narrow furrow between the rows of plants. Michael knelt down and attempted to dig up the plant with his hands but the ground was dry and hard. He would have to get a shovel. He reached down and removed one of his red garters and tied it to the ragweed plant. I've finally fooled the leprechaun, he thought to himself. When I return with a shovel, I'll know exactly where to dig.

Michael ran as fast as his legs would carry him to the nearest farmhouse and borrowed a large garden spade. He was out of breath by the time he returned to the field. And then he could not believe his eyes. There were hundreds of ragweed plants in the field and every one was tied with a red garter just like his.

Many years later—

Patrick O'Shaunessy knew all about leprechauns. His father, Michael O'Shaunessy, his grandfather, his great-grandfather, Tom O'Shaunessy, and even his great-great-great-grandfather had *all* been tricked by one of the little fellows. But Pat knew better. This time he would get the pot of gold. It was time.

The Well-Dressed Vest

Making a vest requires a bit of measuring, cutting, and sewing or stapling. These directions are pretty simple, but you might want to have an adult help you.

With a basic vest and your imagination, you could be almost anything! Play tricks while wearing a leprechaun vest. Be a pirate or a Spanish dancer in a black vest. Make a vest of many colors and act like a silly harlequin. Harlequins are clowns who perform funny stories without words called pantomimes. The Wild West Vest looks a bit weathered, because it's been through cattle drives and more out on the prairie. It's a rugged vest, but you might not be able to resist adding a sprinkle of glitter.

MATERIALS:

1/2 yard of feltlike material

Suggested colors:

*Pirate or Spanish Dancer—
     black*

Wild West Vest—brown

Harlequin—multicolored

Leprechaun—green

ruler

scissors

*needle and thread, or
     stapler*

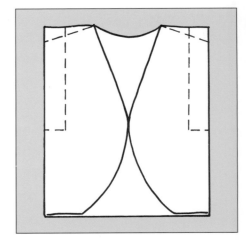

STEPS:

1. *Cut and Fold:* Cut a piece of fabric 18 by 32 inches. Fold in half.

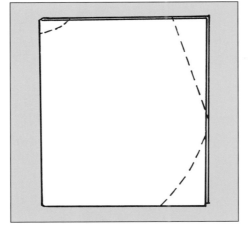

2. *Measure and Cut:* At the top of the folded edge measure down 1 inch and over 3 inches. Make a curved cut. At open edges measure down 9 inches and over 3 inches. Draw a line and cut. Cut a curved edge at the bottom.

3. *Unfold, Measure, and Cut:* Open up fabric and fold cut edges to the center. At side folds measure down 10 inches and across 2 inches. Draw a line and cut. From shoulder edge measure down 1¼ inches. Draw a line and cut. Staple or sew seam and press open.

4. *Decorate:* See ideas below.

Leprechaun

Make the leprechaun vest from green felt. The buttons are cardboard cut in circles and covered with aluminum foil. Buy 6 inches of plastic chain at a crafts or hardware store. Paint it silver.

Wild West Vest

Make the Wild West vest from brown felt. Paint it with fabric paint for a weathered look. Make holes along the edges of the vest with a hole punch, then lace suede cord through the holes. You can get suede cord at a crafts store.

Pirate or Spanish Dancer

The Pirate or Spanish Dancer vest is made out of black felt with black braid sewn along the edges.

Harlequin

For the Harlequin vest, make a vest from black felt. Then cut out diamonds from many colors of felt and glue them onto the black vest with fabric glue.

Isobel Gowdie, known as queen of the Scottish witches, was brought to trial for witchcraft in 1662. In her testimony she described visiting the court of the fairies inside a deep, secret cavern in the hills. She said the interior of the cave was as bright as day, but she did not know the source of the light. She said the Queen of the Fairies was dressed in white linen and the King of the Fairies was very brave.

Brownies never wanted to be seen. There is a story about a group of brownies that helped an old man and woman. They came every night, cleaned up the couple's house, and then skipped back home before dawn. One night the old folks peeked in and saw that the brownies were wearing very tattered clothing. They decided to make them new little suits and caps. On Halloween they put out the new clothing. The brownies were very happy! They put on their new clothes but they knew someone had seen them and they never returned.

CHAPTER SEVEN

Creatures of the Night

Halloween can give you the shivers! Screeching owls, slinking cats, slithery bats, and slimy toads . . . those creepy creatures of the night that make your hair stand on end. In the dark, each one does its part to make Halloween really scary. Here's why.

Cats are said to be witches' companions. This belief probably goes back to the Greek goddess Hecate (HEC-uh-tee), who ruled sorcery. Hecate was sometimes called queen of the witches, and one of her helpers was a cat that had once been a woman.

Historically, witches were said to use cats to do small jobs such as delivering messages to the devil and working spells. These cat helpers were called familiars. Familiars were thought to have their own magical powers such as being able to change into other animals. Witches and their familiars had a special connection—whenever a familiar was hurt, its witch received the same wound.

Some people fear cats because they seem to show such emotions as jealousy, love, and grief and therefore appear to be almost human. The ancient Celts, who lived two thousand years ago, feared cats for this reason. Some say the Celts believed that cats were actually humans under the spell of an evil spirit. Celts feared cats the most during the feast of Samhain, which began on the night of October 31, for this was the night when evil spirits stalked the earth.

Owls also have the reputation of traveling with witches, and some say owls are bad luck. The ancient Romans believed it was a bad omen to see an owl, especially in daylight, because the owl was a messenger of death. The screech of an owl was said to mean death or disaster.

What Became of Them?

He was a rat, and she was a rat,
And down in one hole they did dwell;
And both were as black as a witch's cat,
And they loved one another well.

He had a tail, and she had a tail,
Both long and curling and fine;
And each said, "Yours is the finest tail
In the world, excepting mine."

He smelt the cheese, and she smelt the cheese,
And they both pronounced it good;
And both remarked it would greatly add
To the charms of their daily food.

So he ventured out, and she ventured out,
And I saw them go with pain;
But what befell them I never can tell,
For they never came back again.

Round about the cauldron go;

In the poisoned entrails throw.

Toad, that under the cold stone,

Days and nights has thirty-one

Swelter'd venom sleeping got,

Boil thou first in the charmed pot!

—*Macbeth*, **Shakespeare**

The Bat

Bat, bat, come under my hat,

And I'll give you a slice of bacon;

And when I bake

I'll give you a cake,

If I am not mistaken.

Three Black Cats
(To the tune of "Three Blind Mice")

Three black cats

Three black cats

See how they fly.

See how they fly.

They all climb up on a witch's broom.

They arch their backs and away they zoom.

What a sight to see as they pass the moon.

Three black cats.

Witches kept owls and cats as companions, but they used bats in recipes. Bat blood, wings, and organs were essential ingredients in some deadly ointments and brews. Perhaps witches used bats for sinister recipes because they are naturally rather strange and scary.

Bats spend their days hanging upside down in dark places such as caves. They emerge at dusk and flutter about, using their own high-frequency bat radar to find food. Most bats eat juicy insects, but some need blood to live. Vampire bats live in caves in South and Central America. They were first discovered in the seventeenth century and got their name from the mythic human vampire who sucked others' blood in order to live. Vampire bats eat nothing but blood, for their throats are too narrow for anything but liquid. Vampire bats have sharp, pointed teeth designed to make tiny wounds in small animals, or even humans. They lap up the blood from the little cuts.

Toads were also included in witches' recipes. The Weird Sisters in Shakespeare's *Macbeth* had their own sinister brew, which included an extra-powerful toad—one that had been under a cold stone creating venom in its body for thirty-one days. Long ago people believed that toads were poisonous, because animals and humans had received skin sores from toads. In truth, toads release a burning liquid when threatened by a predator.

Toads are also feared because they are ugly and warty. Toads' warts are glands, and touching them will not cause warts, as many people believe. Toads can fill themselves up with air. This natural ability has been perceived as magical, because it allows toads to puff up or shrink. Toads are also mysterious because they can go for long periods without food. People have told stories of toads living for two to three years without food, buried deep underground. This is impossible, but toads can rest or hibernate in damp places for short periods without nourishment.

Each of the creatures of the night has its role on Halloween night. Cats might be witches' companions, or perhaps witches themselves. Owls provide frightful noises and bad omens. Tiny bats with immense, leathery wings make us want to run, for fear they'll suck our blood. And a hefty, bumpy toad or slippery frog completes a potion, charm, or spell like nothing else. Watch out for these on Halloween!

Bat Bites

Bat Bites are creamy morsels that will send you into blissful fits of super chocolate delight. Get ready to start craving them!

1/2 stick butter or margarine

9-ounce jar crunchy peanut butter

1/2 teaspoon vanilla

1 3/4 cups powdered sugar

1 5/8 cups crispy rice cereal

6-ounce package of chocolate chips

1 tablespoon plus 1 teaspoon vegetable shortening

black cellophane (for bat wings, 10-by-4 inch piece for each Bat Bite)

twist ties (one for each Bat Bite)

black ribbon (to tie up wings, 20 inches for each Bat Bite)

1. Melt butter or margarine in a saucepan over low heat or in a microwave oven.

2. Using an electric mixer, soften or "cream" the peanut butter in a medium-sized bowl. Add the melted butter and the vanilla and beat again.

3. Add sugar and rice cereal to the peanut butter mixture and mix well. Use your hands as this will be very thick.

4. Roll into small balls about 1 inch across. Place on cookie sheet and refrigerate overnight.

5. Melt chocolate chips and shortening in microwave oven or double boiler. Stir until smooth. Dip chilled Bat Bites into chocolate. Place on wax paper until chocolate dries.

Make these Bat Bites especially incredible by wrapping them up in bat wings. Here's how:

1. Cut cellophane into rectangles 10 by 4 inches.

2. Place a Bat Bite in the center of a piece of cellophane.

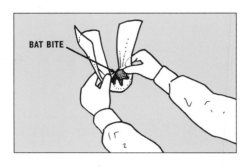

3. Gather the cellophane around the candy beginning with the narrow sides, as shown.

4. Wrap a twist-tie around the top, then make a bow around the tie with the ribbon. The side with the bow will be the front of the Bat Bite.

5. Spread the "wings" out to each side, then cut as shown.

Long Live the King

Hawks that flew over Kilwich Castle could see that it stood on a low hill in the middle of the lush Damona Valley. As they glided on wind currents and soared over the old stone battlements, they observed courtiers and servants milling about in the courtyard. The birds swooped and circled, then flew by the leaded-glass windows of the northern turret, where inside Lady Fiona sat with her needlework by a glowing fire.

She got up, walked to the window, and watched expectantly as two hawks took wing toward the Kildare Forest. "Oh, Thomas," Lady Fiona sighed to her cat, "when will Prince Claudius return from the hunt?"

Perhaps Thomas knew the answer, but he did not say. He rose from a crimson velvet cushion, and with his back to the fire, he stretched his sleek black body. In repose once again, he groomed his thick fur. Lady Fiona admired her cat lovingly and returned to her sewing.

What she did not realize was that the drawbridge had already been lowered for Prince Claudius. He did not come through Kildare Forest as she supposed, but took a shortcut through the ancient Finn burial ground instead. His footmen had just finished helping him from his overburdened horse, the steed heavily laden after the successful hunt. The servants noticed that Prince Claudius was anxious. He left the courtyard stables immediately and took the stairs to the northern turret two and three at a time.

Prince Claudius startled Lady Fiona as he rushed into the quiet room. He was out of breath and his thoughts were muddled. "Fiona, you won't believe what I saw near Finn burial ground. I was just at the entrance when . . . who is Dildrum?"

"Claudius," Lady Fiona said calmly, "what's wrong? And how should I know who Dildrum is? Your face is so flushed, and look at your boots, they're caked with mud." She ushered Prince Claudius to a large curved chair. Together they removed his boots while he caught his breath. Lady Fiona poured wine into a heavy silver goblet and gave it to Prince Claudius. He drank and continued his story.

"I was coming over Narberth Peak, and had stopped at the entrance to the burial ground. It was just growing dark, but through the dim, grainy light I saw the cats. Cats with golden eyes, and fur that looked like, well . . . they looked like that." Prince Claudius gestured toward Thomas, who jumped from his pillow and poised himself at the prince's feet. "They looked just like Thomas!"

"Meow," Thomas responded.

Prince Claudius grew pale. "And they sounded exactly like him, too!"

Lady Fiona smiled at her husband and took his hand. "But, dear," she reassured him, "all cats sound like that. I don't see what is so strange about cats mewing near a graveyard."

Prince Claudius pulled away from Lady Fiona and paced in front of the fireplace. "Fiona, you don't understand—these cats were different. There were nine of them and they walked on their hind legs. Eight carried a small mahogany coffin draped with black velvet, and another one walked in front carrying a bouquet of dark purple roses. A miniature gold crown sparkling with jewels rested on the lid of the little box. Each cat had a white diamond on its chest like . . . exactly like Thomas has on his."

Thomas looked up from his reverie and added, "Meow."

Prince Claudius glanced at his wife fearfully.

"Don't mind Thomas, dear Claudius, carry on with your story."

"The cats marched in time, and with every third step they cried in unison, 'Meow.'"

"Meow," said Thomas in reply.

"Exactly like that!" Prince Claudius exclaimed. "The cats came closer, and I could see their shiny, sleek coats. They held their long, slender tails curled just above the ground. Their eyes were most remarkable, how they shone! Oh, Fiona, their eyes radiated a golden light. The cat who led the procession had the brightest eyes of all, he carried his head high, almost regally. Why he could have been a . . . ."

Prince Claudius paused and looked down at Thomas. The cat stared at the prince with interest and comprehension.

"Thomas seems to enjoy your story as much as I do," Lady Fiona said lightly. "Now, don't look so frightened, Claudius. Thomas couldn't possibly understand. Please, continue. . . . The regal cat in the front was walking . . . ."

With some reluctance, Prince Claudius continued. "They walked toward me, heading for the entrance to the graveyard. They walked silently and solemnly, except with every third step together they cried —"

"Meow," Thomas added.

"Exactly like that!" said Prince Claudius with growing alarm. "The procession halted directly in front of me. I didn't think of riding away. Something about them was familiar, so I remained, and eighteen golden eyes stared at me without blinking. For an instant, I felt charmed. They looked at me like . . . exactly like Thomas stares at me right now!"

Thomas had been observing Prince Claudius intently, but stopped as Lady Fiona picked him up. He purred and rubbed his face against the soft brocade of her sleeve. "Thomas stares at you, Claudius, simply because he loves the sound of your voice. I do so want to hear your story. Please go on, and don't pay attention to him."

Prince Claudius began again. "Well, the lead cat looked at me carefully, then stepped forward cautiously. He gazed up and spoke with a voice much like a purr, and rolling his *r*'s a bit he said, 'Tell Dildrum that Doldrum is dead!' And that is why I asked if you knew Dildrum. How can I tell Dildrum that Doldrum is dead, if I don't know who Dildrum is?"

"Oh, my!" cried Lady Fiona. "Look at Thomas!" And what a sight to see—the cat jumped from her lap and faced the royal couple. As he sat and stared, his chest grew broader, his legs longer, and his tail curled slightly at the end. His eyes grew more radiant and golden. His stare intensified. Finally, the cat cried, "What's this I hear? Old Doldrum dead? Then I, Dildrum, am King of the Cats!"

With that he jumped over the flames in the fireplace, dashed up the chimney, and was never heard from again.

A cat should not be allowed in the same room with a dead body. The cat might be an evil spirit and could change the corpse into a vampire.

A cat sitting with its back to the fire is raising a storm.

You will have good luck if a cat yawns in your presence or rubs against you.

In Ireland, some believe that carrying the bone of a black cat will make a person invisible.

Tea made from a dried cat's liver is said to be a good love potion.

Creepy Mobile

MATERIALS:

1 wire pants hanger with cardboard tube

1 sheet shiny black gift-wrapping cellophane or a black plastic trash bag cut into a rectangle 18 by 30 inches

1 black paper napkin (cocktail size)

black carpet thread

3 3-inch Styrofoam balls

cotton balls

3 paper fasteners

2 9-by-12 inch sheets black construction paper

white glue

black spray or poster paint

silver glitter fabric paint

small jar luminous permanent acrylic paint

small paintbrush

BAT STEPS:

1. *Bend:* Remove cardboard tube from pant hanger. Bend the edges of hanger up to form large arcs on each side.

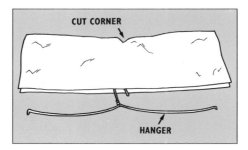

2. *Fold and Cut:* Fold cellophane in half, then in half again. Cut a tiny piece from folded corner. Unfold cellophane and slip top of hanger through this hole.

3. *Glue:* Place hanger on work surface and glue cellophane to wire.

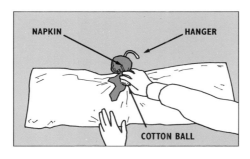

4. *Cut, Stuff, and Sew:* Cut a tiny piece from folded corner of napkin. Unfold and slip top of hanger through hole. Place three cotton balls inside napkin to form bat's head. Tie securely with carpet thread on outside below the cotton to make neck.

5. *Cut:* Cut edge of cellophane to form bat wings. Use two tiny scraps of cellophane to glue onto head to make ears.

6. *Paint:* Streak the wings and neck area with luminous paint, then edge with silver glitter paint. Do not cover luminous paint, as this will prevent it from glowing in the dark.

7. *Paint:* Make eyes and teeth with luminous paint.

SPIDER STEPS:

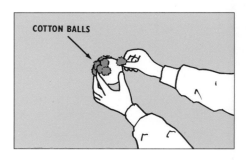

1. *Glue:* Place small amount of white glue on Styrofoam ball. Pull cotton balls apart and glue a little bit at a time to ball. Cover balls completely to get a really furry spider.

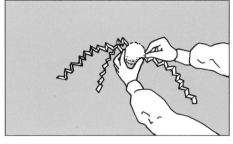

5. *Fold and Glue:* Make ½-inch accordion folds the entire length of strips as shown. Attach legs to body with a dot of glue and a straight pin.

6. *Paint:* Paint on large eyes with luminous paint.

7. *Attach:* Attach spiders to center of hanger and to each side under bat wings.

8. *Light:* Expose mobile to bright light for 30 minutes to activate luminous paint. On Halloween night hang it in a dark place and watch it glowwwwwwwwwwwwww!

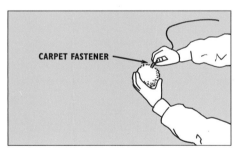

CARPET FASTENER

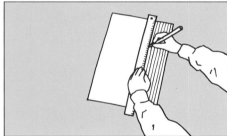

2. *Tie and Insert:* Tie a 10-inch piece of carpet thread to a paper fastener and insert into top of each ball.

3. *Paint:* Spray or brush ball with black paint. Let dry.

4. *Draw, Paint, and Cut:* Draw lines on construction paper every ½-inch as shown. Paint along lines with luminous paint. Allow paint to dry overnight. Cut down middle of the lines to make eighteen ½-inch strips with luminous paint along each edge.

CHAPTER EIGHT

Monster Madness

Frankenstein, Dracula, and the werewolf are probably the most famous Halloween monsters. Their names alone make you think of scary things: the huge Frankenstein monster with his square head; Dracula biting the necks of victims; and the howling werewolf stalking its prey.

Frankenstein is a monster made from body parts of the dead. He is a huge, ugly man with a large forehead, black sunken eyes, and purple scars around his wrists and neck. He's a rather sad creature, because he could never find anyone who truly loved him. Even Dr. Frankenstein, his creator, rejected the awful-looking monster. The lack of love drove the monster to do horrible deeds.

Like Frankenstein, the vampire Count Dracula was a character in a book. According to legend, a vampire is a man or woman who sucks the blood of others in order to survive. Once bitten, the victim is cursed and becomes a vampire. The curse can be broken only if the original vampire is stopped.

A vampire cannot actually be killed, because it is neither dead nor alive. A vampire can be destroyed if it is exposed to sunlight, burned, or kept from getting its life force, blood.

To stop a vampire, a wooden stake made of aspen, maple, or oak must be driven through the vampire's heart while it sleeps. This will pin the vampire to its coffin and keep it from getting the blood it needs to live. The vampire killer must stab its victim with a single stroke—a missed stroke will wake the vampire, who will remove the stake and claim the destroyer as its new victim. A vampire killer must have unwavering concentration and avoid the hypnotizing stare of the vampire. Once under hypnosis, the vampire slayer is powerless.

To make certain a vampire has been destroyed, remove its heart, soak it in oil and vinegar, then shred it and sprinkle it with holy water. Holy water itself can stop a vampire, as will

Three Scary Monsters

Three scary monsters jumping
   on the bed,
   (tap three fingers on palm of opposite hand)

One fell off and bumped its head.
   (one finger falls off, then hold head)

Mama Monster called the doctor
   and the doctor said:
   (hold phone by ear, mime dialing in air)

"No more scary monsters jumping
   on that bed."
   (shake finger)

This old chant was used in a ritual to change a werewolf from wolf form to human form:

Graywolf ugly, graywolf old,

Do at once as you are told.

Leave this man and fly away—

Right away, far away,

Where it's night and never day.

The word "werewolf" itself is very old. It comes from the Old English <u>wer</u>, which means man, and <u>wulf</u>, which means wolf.

The Beastyosaurus

There once was a Beastyosaurus

Who lived when the earth was all porous,

But he fainted with shame

When he first heard his name,

And departed a long time before us.

Please let no Hobgoblins fright me,

No hungry vampires fly in and bite me;

No Witches, Elves, or pesky Ghosts

Visit from their dark outposts.

any other pure substance such as salt or silver. Shooting it with a silver bullet will eliminate a vampire immediately because silver is a pure substance.

Legend says that werewolves are people who turn into wolves because they are under the spell of a witch. Werewolves have long teeth that are red or black, fingers that are short and fat, and hair on their palms. They eat raw meat and are always thirsty. They hate bright light. They are usually covered with scratches and dog bites, which they get while in wolf form.

Werewolves can be men or women, good or evil people. There are families that pass werewolf curses from one generation to the next, while other people are unlucky enough to become a werewolf after being bitten. Some werewolves transform themselves from human form to wolf form by putting on a wolf skin or wolf-skin belt. For others, the werewolf curse changes them into a wolf when the moon is full.

Once in wolf form, a werewolf is not immortal, but they are very strong. A werewolf will viciously attack and eat humans and animals; that is why people hunt them down and kill them. Unlike vampires, werewolves cannot be killed with silver bullets—werewolves laugh at silver bullets. There are many ways to destroy a werewolf, including cutting its forehead three times, throwing clothes at it, and pouring a hot mixture of sulfur, tar, vinegar, and castoreum all over it.

If you wound a werewolf while it is in wolf form, the wound will remain when the werewolf changes back into human form. There's an old story about a farmer who was attacked one night by a huge, vicious wolf. While fighting with the wolf, the farmer cut off the beast's left paw. The wolf howled in pain, then ran off. The farmer staggered home to tell his wife about the attack. As he began describing the story, he noticed bloody bandages around his wife's left hand. Her hand had been mysteriously cut off.

Halloween is a time for monster madness. Which monster suits your personality—a sad, unloved Frankenstein; an evil Dracula, or a ferocious werewolf?

Monster Bash Party Invitations

Take a little time and make your own scary Monster Bash party invitations. Or make cards to send creepy wishes to your friends. This card has three folds, which gives it an extra treat. It's a little tricky to make, so ask for some help.

MATERIALS:

Poster board, black on one side and white on the other, 16 by 7 1/4 inches for each card

orange construction paper (one sheet for each card)

glitter

scissors

glue

black marker or rub-on letters

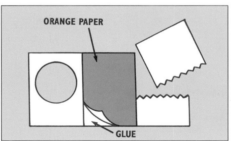

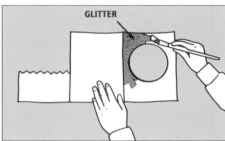

1. *Fold, Draw, Cut:* Fold paper into three sections just like the picture. Draw a circle in the first section, using a circular lid about 4 inches across as a guide. Cut out circle.

2. *Draw and Cut:* About halfway up the third section, draw a zigzag just to the fold of the middle section. Cut along the line to the fold, then along the fold up to the top of the card.

3. *Cut and Glue:* Cut orange paper to fit in the center section and glue to white side of card.

4. *Add Glitter:* Brush glue onto black side of first section (the one with the hole), and sprinkle with glitter.

5. *Draw and Write:* Draw a small black cat in the center orange section. Position the cat so it stands on the fence and is in the middle of the circle. Using rub-on letters or a black marker, write party greeting such as, "Come over and howl!" as well as the date, time, place, and name (if you are giving the party). Or write an eerie message, such as "Watch out for black cats! Happy Halloween!"

A Diary of Life and Death

BASED ON FRANKENSTEIN, BY MARY SHELLEY;
ADAPTED BY CARIN AND JOAN DEWHIRST

Rumors were flying around the medical school about Victor Frankenstein. He had once been a star pupil, but for weeks no one had seen him. Some said he was dead. Others whispered that he was performing strange electrical experiments with dog hearts and cat brains.

Prior to his mysterious disappearance, Victor had not been himself. Usually the very first student to arrive in class, he had started to drag in late, often looking as though he had slept in his clothes. His eyes were black and hollow; his face ghostly pale; he appeared to get thinner by the day. Always an eager participant in class discussions, he was now silent, withdrawn, and strangely disinterested. Folks began to see less and less of him until, finally, several weeks went by when Victor did not show up for class even once. A sort of buzz went through classrooms and corridors as people asked, "Have you seen Frankenstein lately?" No one responded positively. And no one—students or teachers—could guess what Victor Frankenstein was up to.

Fall eased into winter. The days were shorter and the weather chilly and often wet with rain. One morning after an especially violent thunderstorm, Dr. Waldman, professor of electrobiology, decided to visit Victor Frankenstein's apartment. Dr. Waldman had observed Victor in several of his laboratory courses and became concerned early on about his intense, indeed almost bizarre, interest in the field of chemical galvanism. The professor was aware that his young student spent hours and even days experimenting with the use of direct electrical current to stimulate the nerve and muscle tissue of laboratory animals. He had an uneasy feeling that the heightened activity of electrical storms in recent weeks had something to do with Victor's absence from the university. His suspicions were partially confirmed when the landlady at the apartment house informed him that for several months Victor had been spending days and nights in an abandoned watchtower nearby. Following her directions, the professor soon arrived at the entrance to the former lookout post, a badly neglected stone structure.

A worm-eaten door stood partially ajar, so Dr. Waldman stepped inside. He shouted out, "Victor . . . Victor Frankenstein, are you there? It's Waldman here." There was no answer, only shrill squeaks as a large rat ran over the toe of his shoe and attempted to climb up his pant leg. He shivered as he swatted the furry rodent aside. Then he climbed the stairs of the tower. The walls were moist and slippery to his touch and he groped his way cautiously.

A lingering, smoky odor—perhaps singed hair or flesh—made the professor pause at the top of the staircase. He gazed through an open doorway and was astonished to see the enormous array of scientific equipment. His footsteps echoed on the stone floor, sending hundreds of rats scurrying into the far corners of the room. He stiffened with revulsion. This creepy, desolate place was Victor Frankenstein's secret laboratory.

One wall was covered from floor to ceiling with huge electrodes, more anodes and cathodes than Waldman had ever seen in one place. Next to these stood a gigantic air pump, an elaborate galvanic generator, and an immense electrical energy transmitter. He turned to look at the mess in the center of the room—broken test tubes, a smashed microscope, and what looked like an operating table turned on its side. Dozens of surgical tools—scalpels, forceps, and sutures—were strewn all over the floor.

Dr. Waldman cried out, "Victor, Victor, where are you? Are you all right? . . . Please answer me!" But there was only the sound of the wind howling through one of the broken windows in the top floor of the tower.

With his heart pounding, the professor quickly searched the rest of the building. In a tiny alcove at the very top of the tower he found what appeared to be Victor's sleeping quarters. The area held a small bed and a writing table. A chair lay on its side and when Dr. Waldman bent down to pick it up, he spied a small black laboratory manual lying on the floor. His hands trembled as he reached for the book, then he sat down at the desk, slowly opened the manual, and he began to read. . . .

Experiment in Creation
By Victor Frankenstein

August 1: *I am about to embark on an experiment that will change history! At last my years of study at the university and the months of research here in my private laboratory will produce the results I've dreamed about. I am going to create a living human being! But there is so much still to do.*

August 10: *I am beginning to assemble the necessary equipment. It is not an easy task and I have engaged the help of a neighborhood chap named Fritz, whom I have sworn to secrecy. It is imperative that no prying eyes peer into my work.*

September 12: *Fritz has been extremely helpful and the machinery is all in place. It is through this equipment that I will channel the electrical energy from lightning rays to bring life to my creation. I can hardly contain my excitement over this adventure!*

September 27: *I find it more and more difficult to attend classes at the university. Everything seems so boring compared to what I am doing on my own. Fritz and I are starting to collect various body parts from dead corpses.*

October 1: *Rainy and cold today. Went out in late evening with Fritz and found two freshly dug graves. We were pleased with the condition of the bodies.*

October 5: *My laboratory is very cold and Fritz complains, but cold is absolutely essential to maintain the firmness of the fleshy tissues! So far we have been unable to find a brain in proper condition. Fritz is beginning to tire of the work.*

October 9: *At last! On one of our walks Fritz and I stumbled onto a funeral in progress. We waited and watched while the grave digger completed his task. After he left, we quickly dug up the coffin and carted it off to the tower. The brain is perfect...firm and fresh.*

October 21: I have labored day and night, seaming and stitching hands to wrists, feet to legs, arms to shoulders, head to body. My creation is large—nearly eight feet tall by my calculations. I discovered that working with larger parts made my job easier and less tedious. I am racing against time and the seasons as the rainstorms will soon turn into snowstorms and my opportunity will be lost.

October 25: My being is completed! There is no blood, no decay, only the scars of my stitching. I'm sure in time these will disappear. Fritz has left me. The cold plus the isolation, fatigue, and an increasing fear of my work drove him away. So I am alone here in my laboratory with only the rats for company. Their hunger keeps me awake. How they would love to taste my lovely creature! I must fight constantly to keep them off the operating table. But it will all be over soon.

October 28: The weather has been ideal for my experiment! Heavy storms have been arriving daily and within the next few nights I'm sure the force will be strong enough. I can only watch and wait.

October 31: Tonight it will be finished. The wind is howling ferociously outside and the rain is pounding against the windows. All is in readiness. As soon as a bolt of lightning is discharged with sufficient current to charge the apparatus, my creature will be endowed with life. This creation of mine is not dead, even though it is now an accumulation of dead bits and pieces. It is, in truth, a body that has never lived. I will give it that chance!

November 1: One A.M. Just moments ago loud claps of thunder rocked the ground beneath my feet and fierce bolts of lightning charged every cathode in the laboratory. What a spectacle! Sparks flew everywhere. The equipment still hisses and crackles. It seems as though all of heaven opened up and poured out its electrical contents. I watch and wait for my creature to stir, to awaken, to breathe. I am so anxious my head is pounding. As I write this I am observing the first movement. The fingers are twitching, now the arms. . . .

November 1: Four A.M. I have been hiding in my sleeping loft for some time. The details of the last few hours are almost too horrifying to record. The fingers of my creature moved first, slowly and painfully. Then his entire body lurched from left to right. One eyelid popped open, then the other. Soon he rose from the table and looked over at me . . . oh, what horror! What a hideous sight! His eyes were sunken in their sockets. His skin is a sickly yellow and stretched so tight it barely covered the bones and tissues of his face. His lips were black and thin, and from them a strange inhuman sound emerged. He climbed down from the operating table and lunged toward me. I had to flee! Oh, what have I done? I have created this terrible wretch, this ugly monster! How was I to know the powerful electric energy would not only cause the blood to surge through the veins of my creature but under that same force, the solid flesh would melt into such a distorted, hideous, and misshapen figure? I have gone too far! I should never have attempted creation.

November 1: Six A.M. I have been hiding for several hours. For a while I heard much crashing and banging but now all is still. Whoever finds this diary, please know that I will run to the ends of the earth to escape the monster I have created. As I write I sense that a presence . . . someone—something—is standing behind me. Help!!!

Monster Face Pizza

Pretend that you are Dr. Frankenstein and make some monsters. These edible ogres "come to life" in a very, very hot oven, so ask an adult to help you take the hot cookie sheets to and from the oven.

INGREDIENTS FOR FOUR 8 INCH PIZZAS:

4 small ripe tomatoes

1 yellow or bell pepper (mouth)

2 mushrooms (nose)

1 carrot (fangs)

20 basil leaves (hair)

8 black olives (eyes)

4 8-inch Boboli or other prepared pizza breads, tortillas, or pitas

4 tablespoons olive oil

1 cup grated Parmesan cheese

3 cups grated mozzarella cheese

salt and pepper to taste

1. Slice tomatoes into ¼-inch-thick circles. Cut yellow or bell pepper into ¼-inch-wide strips. Thinly slice mushrooms. Cut carrot into fang-shaped pieces. Cut the basil into ¼-inch-wide strips and remove the pits from the olives.

2. Preheat oven to 500 degrees F.

3. Brush pizza breads with one tablespoon of oil, then sprinkle them with Parmesan cheese. Place tomato slices on top and add salt and pepper to taste. Sprinkle mozzarella cheese over tomatoes. Make monster face by adding basil "hair," olive "eyes," mushroom "nose," red pepper "mouth," and carrot "fangs."

4. Bake until cheese is melted and dough has golden edges, about 5 to 8 minutes.

Vampires emerge at nightfall and are especially powerful during a full moon, for they receive strength from the moon.

The corpse of a vampire does not rot or decompose. In olden days, people frequently dug up bodies to make certain they were rotting. If the body was still intact, it was burned in case it was a vampire.

Since a vampire has no soul, it casts no reflection in a mirror.

Vampires are rather smelly and hate any scent stronger than their own. Therefore, to keep vampires away, smear garlic or onion paste on your windowsill or wear a necklace of garlic around your neck.